IDENTITY THEFT

RECLAIMING THE TRUTH OF WHO WE ARE IN CHRIST

TGC

Identity Theft: Reclaiming the Truth of Who We Are in Christ

Published by The Gospel Coalition
2065 Half Day Road
Deerfield, Illinois 60015

Cover design: Trish Mahoney
Typesetting: Ryan Leichty

Printed in the United States of America

ISBN: 978-0-692-13466-5

"I hear all the time that women want to study their identity in Christ. Now there is a book that provides a winsome, biblical, relatable guide for that study! Every chapter in this book is a winner. I can't wait to recommend it!"

NANCY GUTHRIE, author of *Even Better Than Eden: Nine Ways the Bible's Story Changes Everything About Your Story*

"Questions about identity swirl around and in us these days, in the public square, in our churches, and in our homes. The women who have written this book have applied theological truth to the longings and lies in our current cultural moment. A combination of truth and beauty that will make your heart soar."

TREVIN WAX, Director for Bibles and Reference at Lifeway Christian Resources, author of *This Is Our Time* and *Eschatological Discipleship.*

"To know and to live into our identity is essential for both our own well-being and the well-being of the church. With compelling insights and biblical teaching, the essays collected here, written by some of wisest women I know, point out the subtle and significant ways true identity can be lost— and found."

KAREN SWALLOW PRIOR, author of *On Reading Well: Finding the Good Life through Great Books* and *Fierce Convictions: The Extraordinary Life of Hannah More— Poet, Reformer, Abolitionist*

"In a secular world that boasts 50 sexual identities—or 500 by the printing of this commendation—we see that there is no more vital topic for Christians to understand than what identity in Christ means and does. We must ask ourselves:

what is the relationship between my deepest feelings and my sovereign God? Do my compelling desires tell me who I am or how I am? The essays in *Identity Theft* are witty, engaging, accessible, and insightful, with helpful memory verses and study questions, encouraging readers to resist the identity theft of secular modernism and instead to grow in union with Christ."

ROSARIA BUTTERFIELD, author of *The Secret Thoughts of an Unlikely Convert* and *The Gospel Comes with a House Key*

CONTRIBUTORS

HANNAH ANDERSON lives in the Blue Ridge Mountains of Virginia where she spends her days working with her husband in rural ministry, writing, and caring for their family. Her books, *Made for More* and *Humble Roots*, unpack questions of identity and purpose while crafting a vision for the abundant, flourishing life that God promises us through Christ.

LINDSEY CARLSON is a writer, the mother of five, and a native Texan serving in ministry alongside her husband Kyle in Baltimore, Maryland where they recently planted Imprint Community Church. She enjoys teaching and discipling women through writing and public speaking, but most often through the context of the local church.

COURTNEY DOCTOR is an author, Bible teacher, frequent conference and retreat speaker, and periodic blogger. She received her MDiv from Covenant Theological Seminary and is the author of *From Garden to Glory: A Bible Study on the Bible's Story*. Courtney and her husband, Craig, have four adult children and one amazing grandson!

MEGAN HILL is a writer, speaker, and pastor's wife. She serves on the editorial board for Christianity Today, is an editor for The Gospel Coalition website, and is a regular contributor to Today in the Word. The author of *Praying Together: The Priority and Privilege of Prayer: In Our Homes, Communities, and Churches*, Megan lives in Massachusetts with her husband and four children.

JASMINE HOLMES is a Texas native who lives in Jackson, Mississippi with her husband Phillip and her son Wynn. She teaches humanities at a small classical school and attends Redeemer (PCA). She enjoys writing for a variety of ministries but finds her home at jasminelholmes.com.

BETSY CHILDS HOWARD is an editor for The Gospel Coalition. She and her husband, Bernard, live in Manhattan where they recently planted Good Shepherd Anglican Church. She is the author of *Seasons of Waiting: Walking by Faith When Dreams Are Delayed.*

MELISSA KRUGER serves as an editor for The Gospel Coalition and on staff as Women's Ministry Coordinator at Uptown Church (PCA) in Charlotte, North Carolina. She's the author of *The Envy of Eve: Finding Contentment in a Covetous World, Walking with God in the Season of Motherhood,* and *In All Things: A Nine Week Devotional on Unshakeable Joy.* Her husband, Mike, is the president of Reformed Theological Seminary and they have three children.

JEN POLLOCK MICHEL lives with her husband and five children in Toronto where they attend Grace Toronto Church. She is the author of *Teach Us to Want* and *Keeping Place* and frequently travels to speak at churches and conferences.

TRILLIA NEWBELL is the author of *Enjoy: Finding the Freedom to Delight Daily in God's Good Gifts, Fear and Faith: Finding the Peace Your Heart Craves, United: Captured by God's Vision for Diversity* and a children's book, *God's Very Good Idea: A True Story of God's Delightfully Different Family.* She is currently Director of Community Outreach for the Ethics and Religious Liberty Commission for the Southern Baptist Convention. Trillia and her husband Thern reside with their two children near Nashville, Tennessee.

JEN WILKIN is an author and Bible teacher from Dallas, Texas. Her passion is to see others become articulate and committed followers of Christ, with a clear understanding of why they believe what they believe, grounded in the Word of God. She is the author of *Women of the Word* and *None Like Him*.

IDENTITY THEFT

RECLAIMING THE TRUTH OF WHO WE ARE IN CHRIST

INTRODUCTION: WHO AM I?

MELISSA KRUGER

My junior year of college, I walked into my apartment, mentally preparing for what I assumed would be an awkward conversation. I wasn't sure about what I was going to say, but I knew I needed to talk to my friend. Confrontation is never easy, and in this situation, I'll admit I felt like perhaps I was making a mountain out of a molehill.

My friend had been using a fake ID to get into college parties with her sorority sisters. While she wasn't using it to drink alcohol, she was assuming someone else's identity each time she went out with her friends. Her intentions were good (to build relationships with her non-believing sorority sisters), but her means involved telling a lie to do so.

The conversation went much better than I anticipated, and my roommate graciously responded to my fumbling attempts to explain my concerns. She agreed what she was doing was dishonest and threw away her fake ID.

At some point or another, we've probably all assumed an identity not our own. As children, most of us played dress-up and pretended to be doctors, teachers, builders, veterinarians, and superheroes. Others have acted in plays or transformed into a favorite character for a costume party. Pretending to be someone else for an evening can be pretty fun. However, there's always the understanding that tomorrow will come, and we'll go back to being ourselves.

The problem arises when we dress ourselves up with counterfeit identities and wear them on a regular basis. We believe we aren't enough, so we find ways to make ourselves appear better. Some do this in their work environment—one recruitment firm estimates that 40 percent of all resumes contain false information, including dishonesty about age, experience, education, and previous salaries.[1] Others do this in subtle ways by exaggeration, self-promotion, or spreading gossip (tearing others down to elevate themselves). The fear of not being enough overflows into false living.

There's also the opposite reality that someone may attempt to steal our identity. In college, my wallet was stolen while I was out of town on vacation. As soon as I noticed it was missing, I called to cancel my credit card. However, when my statement arrived, I realized someone used my credit card to go on a massive shopping spree. I felt vulnerable, angry, and powerless all at the same time. I was an early victim of a problem that has only grown over the past 20 years—identity theft. In 2016, more than 15 million people were victims of stolen identity, with a total loss of $16 billion.[2]

Fake IDs, padded resumes, and identity theft aren't just societal problems. They represent our spiritual struggles with identity. Sometimes we knowingly live duplicative lives: we

1   "Most Common Resume Lies," Forbes, May 23, 2006, https://www. forbes.com/2006/05/20/resume-lies-work_cx_kdt_06work_0523lies. html#7ceb260878b5.

2   "Identity Fraud Hits Record High with 15.4 Million U.S. Victims in 2016, Up 16 Percent According to New Javelin Strategy & Research Study," Javelin, February 1, 2017, https://www.javelinstrategy.com/ press-release/identity-fraud-hits-record-high-154-million-us-vic-tims-2016-16-percent-according-new.

act one way with one group of people and quite differently with another group. Other times, we put on a pleasant
Christian exterior, but inside we're angry, bitter, and boiling
over with frustration at God and others. We're also prone
to becoming victims of identity theft in a spiritual sense:
the Devil seeks to steal, kill, and destroy us with his lies
and accusations.

Our three enemies—the world, the flesh, and the Devil—all seek to discourage and dishearten us from living in the
fullness of who we are in Christ. The world wants to conform us into its mold, our flesh craves self-glory, and Satan
reminds us of past sins and present failings in an attempt to
paralyze our faith.

I wish putting on our true identity were as simple as my
roommate tossing out her fake ID. But in reality, it's a battle.
It's a struggle to remember who we are in Christ. We need
a biblical understanding of identity to guard our hearts and
minds as we seek to walk in a manner worthy of the Lord.

Who does the Bible tell me I am in Christ? This is the
question we'll explore in this book. Each chapter we'll consider our identity in three ways:

- Identity theft: Expose our false notions of identity.
- Identity truth: Understand the biblical truth of our
  identity in Christ.
- Identity transformed: Reflect on what it looks like to
  live in our new (and true) identity.

I always find it helpful to discuss concepts like this with
others, so I'm thankful for the various voices you'll be
hearing from in this book. Each of these contributors has
a passion for Jesus and a love for people. They write with
profound theological insight, biblical knowledge, and
practical application.

At the end of each chapter, we've provided study questions if you decide to grab some friends and chew on these concepts together. We've also offered a verse to memorize at the end of each chapter. There's no better way to guard our minds than hiding Scripture in our hearts to correct and rebuke the lies we tell ourselves. Take the time to memorize these passages to remind you—day after day, week after week—of who you are in Christ.

To that end, the main emphasis of this book is not focused on who we are specifically as women. Many have written with skill and insight considering how the Scriptures speak to us as women. This book attempts to back up a step and reflect upon the question: *Who am I in Christ?*

As author and missionary Elisabeth Elliot expressed, "The fact that I am a woman does not make me a different kind of Christian, but the fact that I am a Christian makes me a different kind of woman."[3] Our identity in Christ is a fixed anchor guiding us through the changing seasons and circumstances of our lives as women. We're not primarily defined by our college degree, marital status, the number of children we have, where we live, or the work we do. It's our identity in Christ that shapes every aspect of our lives. As Paul told the Colossians, "He is before all things, and in him all things hold together" (Col. 1:17). Understanding who we are in Christ impacts every other area of our lives.

Let's dig in—we have life-changing truths to consider. Our prayer is for you to experience the fullness of life offered to you in Christ. Don't waste your life on lesser pursuits. As you read, may you increasingly know God's plan for you in Jesus:

---

3   Elisabeth Elliot, *Let Me Be a Woman* (Carol Stream, Illinois: Tyndale, 1976), 43.

But you are a chosen race, a royal priesthood, a holy nation, a people for his own possession, that you may proclaim the excellencies of him who called you out of darkness into his marvelous light. Once you were not a people, but now you are God's people; once you had not received mercy, but now you have received mercy. (1 Pet. 2:9-10)

CHAPTER 1

FREE: RESCUED BY GRACE

JEN WILKIN

To serve God, to love God, to enjoy God,
is the sweetest freedom in the world.[1]
—Thomas Watson

When you think of freedom, what's the first thing that comes to mind? For me, it's La Jolla Cove and a snorkeling adventure that quickly went from fun to frantic. The story involves no shark attacks or near-drownings; no, instead, my dark moment of captivity happened when I tried to remove

---

[1]   Thomas Watson, *The Christian Soldier* (New York: Robert Moore, 1816), 115, https://play.google.com/books/reader?id=XJx-HAAAAYAAJ&printsec=frontcover&output=reader&hl=en&pg=GBS.PA115.

my wetsuit in a public bathroom. To be precise, it was a borrowed wetsuit, and its owner was about six inches shorter than I am. The thing with wetsuits is that they slip on fairly easily when they are dry. Getting out of them once they're wet takes strength and technique, neither of which I possessed. And the too-small size didn't help.

Having extracted my head from the neck opening with enormous difficulty, I began pulling my arms out of the sleeves, turning them inside out as I tugged. Instead of coming free, my arms got stuck, pulled close into my chest, with my hands trapped inside the sleeves. My adrenaline surged, and I could feel a shriek welling up inside my chest as I began flailing and gasping for breath. Some combination of unconsciousness and public humiliation seemed imminent. Just as I was about to run screaming into the daylight, my daughters appeared in the doorway and performed a laborious extraction. Free! I will never forget the exuberant relief as that dripping pile of nefarious neoprene was peeled away.

Perhaps no idea is more foundational to the Christian's identity than freedom. The good news of the gospel is that we are no longer slaves to unrighteousness but are free—free from the bondage brought about by the fall, free to be who God created us to be. But the exact nature of that freedom can evade us, even causing us to doubt if we have truly received it. Our initial moment of the euphoric relief of conversion fades, and we once again struggle in the straight-jacket of sins we thought we'd stripped off for good. This has certainly been my story.

WHERE'S THE FREEDOM?

I grew up in the Bible Belt where, by mid-elementary, most of my peers could point proudly to a note written in the front of their Bibles announcing the exact date they Got

Saved. At junior-high youth rallies the rededications began, along with a smattering of I-thought-I-was-saved-but-I-really-wasn'ts (scribble over that first date and write in the new one). Through all seven verses of "Just as I Am," and all four years of high school, we children of the Bible Belt battled our doubts and bustled our backslidden selves down aisles to altar rails.

Maybe, we thought, *this time just maybe The Saving will stick.*

Our problem was this: our sinning had not ceased with our professions of faith. The salvation that had promised us new life in Christ had by all appearances failed to deliver. We still made all the same mistakes, and along the thorny path of adolescence we added fresh failures to the list. Damning evidence, or so we thought, that when we Prayed The Prayer we had somehow not done it right. Where was the freedom from sin we had been promised?

Looking back, I wonder if for many of us, our problem was not with salvation itself, but with our understanding of how salvation brings freedom. Not until my early 20s did I gain any clarity on this issue. I knew I served a God who *was and is and is to come*, but I had yet to learn that I possessed from him a salvation of which the same could be said. Salvation from sin can be broken down into three categories: justification, sanctification, and glorification. For the believer, our justification *was*, our sanctification *is*, and our glorification *is to come*. We were saved, we are being saved, we will be saved. I've found the easiest way to understand these three forms of freedom is to remember the three Ps: penalty, power, and presence.

Without a firm grasp of these concepts, we can remain trapped in an old identity. Understanding God's work in us and through us is foundational to our understanding of who he created us to be. Every other aspect of identity that we'll study in this book flows from God's redemptive work in our lives. Just as I found myself trapped inside a wet suit that wouldn't let me go, we need someone to free us to become who we were intended to be. God's rescue begins with our justification.

JUSTIFICATION: FREEDOM FROM SIN'S PENALTY

When we came to saving faith in Christ, confessing our great need of him and asking for forgiveness from the punishment we deserved, we were met with God's unequivocal "yes." Since Christ bore the penalty for our sins, we received freedom from that penalty for all sins past, present, and future. We were justified before God our judge because our penalty had been paid. Those who have been justified never need re-justifying. We can look back to the time of our justification (perhaps written in the front of our Bible?) and know that there is no condemnation for those who are in Christ Jesus (Rom. 8:1–2).

Our justification is behind us. We *were saved* from sin's penalty, miraculously freed from its death sentence.

SANCTIFICATION: FREEDOM FROM SIN'S POWER

Now that the grace of God has been set upon us as a permanent seal (2 Cor. 1:20–22), we are being made new. We are being set free from the power of sin by the power of the Spirit. God's grace is restoring to us a will that wants what he wants. Before we were justified, our broken wills were utterly subject to the power of sin. We chose sin at every turn. Even when we made choices that appeared good from an external standpoint, because we had no higher internal purpose than to glorify self, these choices were ultimately sinful as well.

Now, the power of sin is broken. We've been given the deposit of the Holy Spirit. Though we once chose only to sin, now we have the power (and the growing desire) to choose righteousness. We who were once slaves to sin's power are now free to serve God. We don't always use our freedom. We still sin, but over time we learn increasingly to choose holiness. Our entire lives from that handwritten date in our Bibles onward are devoted to "working out our salvation" (Phil. 2:12–13) as we learn to choose righteousness instead of sin, to walk in obedience to God's commands.

Our sanctification is ongoing. It's a slow-moving growth in holiness. We *are being saved* from sin's power, increasingly free from its pull.

GLORIFICATION: FREEDOM FROM SIN'S PRESENCE

We will fight to grow in holiness our entire earthly lives. But when we have run the race and fought the good fight, we will enter into the presence of the Lord forever. We will be glorified. In his presence, our soul rest will at last be complete, as sin and its devastation will cease to assail us. There can be no evil in his presence. Though now we are surrounded on all sides by sinfulness, though now sin continues to cling to our hearts, on a day not too distant we will go to a place where sin is no more. In our glorification we will at last be granted freedom from the very presence of sin. At that moment, for the first time, we will rightly reflect our true identity in every fiber of our being.

Our glorification is coming. It's the day we trade the persistent presence of sin for the perfect presence of the Lord. We *will be saved* from sin's presence, completely free at last.

FALSE FREEDOM

It's possible not just to doubt our freedom, but to presume upon it in sinful ways. This, too, is an identity crisis of sorts. If we misunderstand our past *freedom from sin's penalty* as a "get out of jail free" card, we may lapse into the false freedom of *license*, relaxing God's commands instead of resting in Christ's perfect obedience to them. We may be tempted to "sin all the more that grace may abound." Those of us who wear our past failures openly and often succumb to shame may be particularly tempted by the false freedom of license.

If we misunderstand our progressive *freedom from sin's power* as something achieved by our own efforts, we may lapse into the bondage of *legalism* instead of godly obedience. We may confuse Spirit-enabled change with the false freedom of self-improvement and moralism. Those of us whose besetting sin is pride, those who are good at keeping up appearances and following the rules, may be particularly tempted by the false freedom of legalism.

If we misunderstand our future *freedom from sin's presence* as a means of escaping suffering, we may lapse into the bondage of *escapism* instead of eager anticipation. There is a difference between being prepared for the Lord's return and being anxious for it. Every hardship, health concern, or heartache causes us to long for the day when these things are no more. But if a fixation on future freedom causes us to trade patience and steadfastness for a fretful "Are we there yet?" we trade trusting the Lord for questioning his timing. God is not slow in keeping his promises. Those enduring trial are particularly (and understandably) tempted by the false freedom of escapism.

Instead of embracing false freedoms, we are called to "Live as people who are free, not using your freedom as a cover-up for evil, but living as servants of God" (1 Pet. 2:16).

REST, LABOR, HOPE

If my childhood peers and I had better understood the past, present, and future aspects of salvation's freedom, we might have saved ourselves a great deal of anxiety and a few trips down the aisle. The knowledge that sin is gradually overcome across a lifetime would have been good news to the teenager who thought her ongoing sin invalidated her profession. The knowledge that sanctification is hard work would have helped her topple the myth of the effortless stock-photo Christian life. The knowledge that total freedom from sin is a future certainty would have helped her ask in faith for grace for her current failures and wait patiently in trials.

Maybe you, too, have found salvation mystifying. Maybe you've wondered, *If I'm really saved, why don't I feel fully free?* Well, you're not yet fully free, but you will be. Our complete freedom from sin is certain, but it's not sudden. So we rest confidently in our justification, we labor diligently in our sanctification, and we hope expectantly in our glorification.

Be assured of your justification. It *was*. One day, you were freed fully from the penalty of sin.

Be patient with your sanctification. It *is*. Each day, you are being freed increasingly from the power of sin.

Be eager for your glorification. It *is to come*. One day, you will be freed finally from the presence of sin.

For today, remember: Christ is in you and you are in him. Your identity is securely anchored even as you are increasingly being transformed. Sister in Christ, live each day in the joyful certainty that "if the Son sets you free, you will be free indeed" (John 8:36).

VERSE TO MEMORIZE

*For freedom Christ has set us free; stand firm there-
fore, and do not submit again to a yoke of slavery.*

Galatians 5:1

QUESTIONS FOR GROUP DISCUSSION

OPENING QUESTION: You've probably heard a statement like this: "I'm free to be me, and you're free to be you." What do people mean when they say that? Is it true? Why or why not?

1. When you think of freedom, what's the first thing that comes to mind?

2. READ ROMANS 6.

   a. How does this passage describe our justification? What has already been done for us?

   b. How does this passage describe our sanctification? How is God working in us now?

   c. How does this passage describe our glorification? What are we promised will happen?

3. How is the Christian understanding of freedom different from the world's understanding of freedom?

4. Why is it sometimes difficult to believe we're freed from sin's penalty and power? In what ways do you battle to believe you're free from sin's penalty? From sin's power?

5. Are you more tempted to license, legalism, or escapism in the Christian life? Why?

6. READ 1 PETER 2:16. In what ways can we use the concept of freedom as cover-up for evil?

7.   READ GALATIANS 5:1 AND 5:13–24.

     a.   What do you learn about true freedom from this chapter?

     b.   What does it look like to live by the flesh (as a slave)?

     c.   What does it look like to live freely (by the Spirit)?

8.   How is living in the freedom of the gospel the foundation for our identity? How does the gospel offer truth about our identity and hope for our identity?

9.   As you think back over the chapter, what particular truth struck you? How will you live differently in light of that new understanding?

CHAPTER 2

REFLECTION: MADE IN GOD'S IMAGE

HANNAH ANDERSON

Without knowledge of self there is no knowl-
edge of God . . . without knowledge of
God, there is no knowledge of self.[1]
—John Calvin

You'd think, after having lived with myself my whole life, that I'd be able to predict my likes and dislikes, that a lifetime of experience would result in some level of self-knowledge. But I have found this is rarely the case. Take, for example, a

---

1   John Calvin, *Institutes of the Christian Religion*, trans: Henry Beveridge (London: Arnold Hatfield for Bonham Norton, 1599), Book 1, Chapter 1, http://www.reformed.org/books/institutes/books/book1/bk1ch01.html.

recent event in our family that made me question everything I thought I knew about myself.

For months, my 11-year-old son had been begging for a cat. We had a beagle a few years earlier, but our lifestyle and love of travel (along with the beagle's lifestyle and love of travel) meant we spent the majority of our time together either trying to find a dog sitter or trying to find the dog. I wasn't eager to return to caring for a pet, but who was I to say no to a young boy with blue eyes? So, a few weeks before Christmas, he and I went to the local animal shelter and came home with a beautiful, long-haired black-and-white cat named Francis.

The first thing Francis did was to take up residence on my bed.

Having not grown up with inside pets, I didn't take this well. I did not like the thought of cat hair on my comforter, of breathing cat dander while I slept, of cat paws waking me in the morning. I promptly filled my Amazon cart with lint rollers, an air purifier, an essential oil diffuser, and disinfecting wipes. I also bought cat litter, food, and a collar. I moaned over the amount of money I was spending, calculated upcoming vet bills, and generally felt like a martyr to my son's desire.

But then something happened. My next shopping trip included a cat care book, scratching post, memory foam cat bed, and toys filled with catnip. I worried when Francis was out after dark. I'd get up in the middle of the night when I remembered his water bowl was empty. When the kids were off at school, I'd invite him to sit with me in my favorite chair. I began to watch cat videos on YouTube.

Then one night, I could deny it no longer. "I think," I whispered to my husband as we lay in the darkness of our bedroom, the night shrouding our secrets "I think I might be . . . a cat person."

IDENTITY THEFT

Coming to terms with my appreciation for Francis was one of the less significant discoveries of my adult life, although it was startling in its own way. There have been so many other truly seismic moments of self-discovery over the years that I'm hardly surprised any more when I find that a long-held category of identity has shifted. It unsettled me at first though.

Throughout childhood my fairly stable sense of self was built primarily on my family, school, and church. Venturing into early adulthood, I remained generally confident in my new roles and calling. But then bit by bit, with each new responsibility, my sense of self seemed to waver and with it my confidence. Instead of becoming more sure of myself as I grew older, I felt uncertain, at times even listless.

I looked for things to ground my identity in—was it found in my roles? Was it in my gifting? Was it in my personality, that intangible self revealed by the endless stream of psychological tests I took online? Who was I, really?

In the midst of our confusion, people often turn to categories to give us a sense of who we are. We sort ourselves by age, gender, economic class, ethnicity, relationship status, and yes, even whether we prefer cats and dogs. Somehow knowing I'm a pastor's wife, mother of three, and author who lives in the Blue Ridge Mountains of Virginia gives me a sense of where I fit in the world. While these categories are helpful, they're limited. Our reliance on them can cause us even more confusion. Researchers call this tendency to find our identity in social categories "identity politics." This term is not limited to government or policy debates but speaks more broadly to how we center our sense of self on one particular attribute of our identity and then define everything else by it.

To be fair, categories themselves are not wrong. We use the categories of occupation, relationship, family, and geography to communicate how we spend our days and the work we have been called to on this earth. The problem comes when we ask these categories to do more than they can do—when we ask them to hold all that we are. After all, if we try to stuff complicated, diverse, fully formed living beings into small, inanimate categories, we shouldn't be surprised when they feel tight and cramped and begin to suffocate us.

Worse still, when we define ourselves with limited categories, any shift in those categories can destabilize our sense of self. What happens to us when life doesn't play out the way we expected—when a marriage ends or never happens in the first place? What happens to us when we're laid off or fail in the marketplace? What happens to us when motherhood doesn't come easily?

If we've invested our sense of self in something small, temporal, and unstable, we will become small, temporal, and unstable people. When they collapse or come to a natural end (as even good things do), we enter a crisis of identity. For without them, how will we know our sense of purpose, calling, and direction? Life will become meaningless and empty.

In an essay entitled "The New Midlife Crisis: Why (and How) It's Hitting Gen X Women," author and essayist Ada Calhoun writes about the despair and confusion women can experience when the categories they rely on either shift or disappoint them.[2] Highlighting women who have been encouraged to focus their identity on the marketplace, Calhoun notes that after decades of pursuing corporate success,

---

2   Ada Calhoun, "The New Midlife Crisis: Why (and How) Its Hitting Gen X Women," Oprah.com, accessed March 15, 2018, http://www.oprah.com/new-midlife-crisis.html.

women can find themselves laid off, underemployed, or simply unsatisfied. To cope many are tempted to quit their jobs; abuse food, alcohol, and prescription drugs; and even engage in risky flirtations and affairs—all to try to answer this deeper question of who they are and where they fit in the world.

Lest we're tempted to blame the crisis of identity on corporate structures, women devoted to more domestic endeavors can experience the same loss of self because our roles as wives and mothers—as good and as necessary as they may be—are also limited and temporal. Think about the loss of purpose women can experience when, after decades of caring for them, children leave the nest. Or even before that. Have you ever wondered why we can be so quick to react when someone corrects our child? Or why we judge each others' lifestyle choices and why we feel judged by theirs?

If we look below the surface, we'll most likely discover we've somehow begun to center our sense of self on our children, our family, or even our particular theological convictions. Discussions about these things will end up feeling personal because we've made them personal by investing our sense of wholeness so deeply in a particular choice that we cannot risk it being challenged or confronted. To lose it is to lose our self.

IDENTITY TRUTH

The truth about our core identity is so much richer, more glorious, and more soul-satisfying than any category or role we could conceive for ourselves. Were we to write the script of our lives it would likely reflect the bland mediocrity that comes from playing it safe. But God, whose ways are far above ours, who does beyond what we can ask or think, calls us to find ourselves in something more than earthly categories. He calls us to find our identity in him.

In Genesis 1, Scripture tells us God made mankind in his own image, "in the image of God he created him, male and female he created them" (1:27). Of all this means, it first means that our deepest sense of self must be found in God. Not in categories, not in roles, not in successes or failure. In him.

Because by making us in his image, God did more than simply confer value on our lives; he also instilled in us a deep sense of purpose and calling. In the ancient world, an image reflected and represented a sovereign king. Often stamped on coins or made into statues, the image of the king showed his glory, power, and might. It reminded citizens in the farthest reaches of the kingdom that they existed under both his protection and also his rule. It was meant to inspire awe and authority.

As image bearers of God, we too are called to show forth the glory, power, and might of our King. Our deepest sense of purpose and identity is so bound up in this calling that everything about our lives—from the work we do, to the people we love, to the place we live—all somehow connect back to him. As Augustine confessed, "Thou hast formed us for Thyself, and our hearts are restless til they find rest in Thee."[3]

Nothing less than God will satisfy you. Nothing less will sustain you. Nothing less will suffice.

But even as we begin to find our sense of identity in him, we can quickly be tempted to want to actually *be* God. We can develop a sense of self that convinces us that we are stronger, more capable, wiser, and more powerful than we

---

3   Augustine, *Confessions*, trans. Edward B. Pusey (Collier Books), book 1, chap. 1, http://www.leaderu.com/cyber/books/augconfessions/bk1.html.

actually are. We can believe that categories are meant to be broken, that nothing can contain us, that we are limitless. In other words, we can begin to confuse our created identity with God's identity as our Creator.

In Genesis 3, just a few short chapters after the Scripture reveals our calling as image bearers, we see the first man and woman reject their God-given identity when they rejected his authority over them. Tempted by the serpent's promise that they would become "like God" himself, they reached out for the forbidden fruit of the tree of the knowledge of good and evil and ate. They reached out for independence, self-determination, and freedom but instead grasped only sorrow, confusion, and death.

In taking the fruit, the man and woman did more than simply cross a line marked "Do Not Touch." They denied the authority and power of their King. Instead of representing his power and glory as an image is meant to do, they sought power and glory for themselves. They mounted an insurrection.

To be an image bearer—to be who we were created to be—we must first submit ourselves to the authority of our King.

God's invitation to experience life in him does not negate that he is the source of our life. His kindness to allow us to experience his glory does not mean we can steal it from him. "I am the LORD," he declared in Isaiah 42:8, "that is my name; my glory I give to no other." And Jude 25 confirms that we sing praise "to the only God, our Savior, through Jesus Christ our Lord," and to him belong "glory, majesty, dominion, and authority, before all time and now and forever." As clearly as God has established the boundaries of our identity, he guards and protects the boundaries of his.

Like the first man and woman, we too can easily be lifted up with pride and the desire to be God. It's often subtle, but every time we presume to live outside our given limits, every time we obey a voice other than his, every time we insist on working in our own strength and for our own glory, we deny the truth of who he is and who we are as his image bearers. Instead of reflecting *his* power and glory, we seek power and glory for ourselves. Instead of reflecting his rule, we buck it. Consumed with pride, we refuse to know him and as a result cannot truly know ourselves.

But God will not leave us to destroy ourselves or the world he has made. In his kindness and mercy, he comes to redeem all we have lost and teach us how to be the people he has made us to be. It begins by remembering who we are and who he is as our God.

In Philippians 2:6–8, Paul tells us that out of his deep humility, Christ Jesus—despite being in the form of God— "did not count equality with God a thing to be grasped, but emptied himself, by taking the form of a servant, being born in the likeness of men. And being found in human form, he humbled himself by becoming obedient to the point of death, even the death on a cross."

When Jesus willingly took on the limits of our human identity, when he became obedient to the Father, he restored our true identity as image bearers. All the first Adam lost was redeemed through the last. And as we encounter him, as "we become fully aware of our condition as creatures" to quote the philosopher Dietrich von Hildebrand, it will "fling from us the last particle of self-glory."[4] We will once again be able to live as we ought, to be who we truly are.

This is the paradox of finding identity in Christ: In order to become our truest selves, in order to know ourselves,

---

4   Dietrich Von Hildebrand, *Humility: Wellspring of Virtue* (Manchester NH: Sophia Institute Press, 1997), 24.

we must know him. In order to reflect his goodness and glory, we must be made like him, we must be "renewed in knowledge after the image of [our] creator" (Col. 3:10). We may lose our lives in the process—we may be stripped of everything we knew to be true about ourselves. But in doing so, in losing our lives for his sake, we will find them. In surrendering to God, we will experience the full, abundant life that only he can offer as the Creator of life.

In God's wisdom, our identity as image bearers simultaneously elevates and humbles us. It reminds us our calling is too grand and too glorious to be contained in human categories. But it also confronts our pride by reminding us we are not God. In this sense, finding identity as image bearers centers us, putting us in our place in the best possible way.

IDENTITY TRANSFORMED

You may find as you begin to center your identity more fully on God that little about your life changes—at least externally. Most likely, you will still use certain categories to explain how you spend your days. You will work your job, love your family, and serve others. But while life around you may not change, centering your identity on God will make you a different person in it.

And when changes do come—an illness that prevents you from caring for those you love, the loss of income that requires downsizing, the cross-country move that strips you of friends and family, the death of a marriage, death itself— instead of these changes shattering your sense of identity, you will find them transforming it. Each new challenge, each shifting role is a tool in the hand of God to shape you into the image bearer you are meant to be. As C. S. Lewis wrote in his classic *Mere Christianity*:

> He will make the feeblest and filthiest of us . . . into
> a dazzling, radiant, immortal creature, pulsating all
> through with such energy and joy and wisdom and
> love as we cannot not imagine, a bright stainless mir-
> ror which reflects back to God perfectly (though, of
> course, on a smaller scale) His own boundless power
> and delight and goodness. The process will be long
> and in parts very painful, but that is what we are in for.
> Nothing less.[5]

In moments of difficulty, confusion, and loss, God is strip-
ping you of all the things you may reach out for instead of
him. He is cutting and cleaning and crafting your life so it
can shine the light of his glory. Do not be afraid when this
happens. Do not be afraid when the questions come and the
things you once relied on don't satisfy you any longer. Do
not be afraid when he comes to relieve you of your idols of
identity. Do not be afraid because a good and powerful God
is at work. He is coming to reclaim his own, and he will not
stop until you become your truest self—a woman whose life
reflects the greatness and glory of her God.

---

5   C. S. Lewis, *Mere Christianity* (Nashville: Broadman and Holman
Publishers, 1996), 176.

VERSE TO MEMORIZE

And we all, with unveiled face, beholding the glory of the Lord, are being transformed into the same image from one degree of glory to another.

2 Corinthians 3:18

QUESTIONS FOR GROUP DISCUSSION

OPENING QUESTION: Have you ever taken a personality test—whether in a magazine survey, a Facebook article, or for your workplace environment? Why do you think we enjoy taking these tests?

1.   What are areas we tend to consider as core to our identity? How do we see this in the way we introduce ourselves or introduce others?

2.   Have you ever had a situation when the question of "Who am I?" felt unclear or in question because of a change in your circumstances or understanding? How did that experience shape or change you?

3.   READ GENESIS 1:26–27. What is significant about being made in the image of God? How does it differentiate humans from the rest of God's creation? How does it affect how you view others?

4.   READ ROMANS 5:5–21.

   a.   While we are made in the image of God, because of Adam's sin, we bear the brokenness of his transgressions. Apart from Christ, how does this passage describe us?

   b.   What does this passage tell us that Christ has done for us?

   c.   Compare the free gift of God to the trespass of Adam. What similarities do you notice? What differences?

5. READ EPHESIANS 4:20–5:2.

    a.   What does it look like to live as an imitator of God?

    b.   How is it possible for us to live out this calling?

6. How does centering our identity in Christ provide stability to our sense of self, even as our seasons and circumstances change? What truths about our identity in Christ are unchanging?

7. How have you seen change—sometimes difficult and unwanted—lead to God's transformation in your life? How has that at times been a difficult, but needed transformation?

8. As you think back over the chapter, what particular truth resonated with you? How will you live differently in light of that new understanding?

CHAPTER 3

CHILD: BELOVED BY THE FATHER

COURTNEY DOCTOR

*If you want to judge how well a person under-
stands Christianity, find out how much he makes
of the thought of being God's child, and having
God as his Father. If this is not the thought that
prompts and controls his worship and prayers and
his whole outlook on life, it means that he does
not understand Christianity very well at all.[1]*
—J. I. Packer

I can't carry a tune but love to sing. I love singing songs that
proclaim God's goodness, majesty, sovereignty, mercy, power,

---

1   J. I. Packer, *Knowing God* (London: Hodder and Stoughton,
1973), 182.

and faithfulness. Music stirs my affections and directs my soul to my Creator. But there is one song that always astounds me: *How He Loves* by David Crowder.[2] You may be familiar with it; the first verse and chorus proclaim:

> And I realize . . . how great your affections are for me.
> And, oh, how He loves us, oh,
> Oh, how He loves us,

What astounds me is that this is not a song where we declare *our* love for *God*. This is a song where we stand and declare God's love for us—and not just declare it, but bask, revel, and delight in it. No other religion in the world can do this. Christianity is the only faith that would dare stand and boldly repeat, "How great *your* affections are for *me*. Oh, how he loves us." Declarations of love typically travel the other direction—from the giver to the receiver(s). But here, the receivers of love declare confidence and joy in the sure knowledge that a perfect love, from a perfect Father, has been lavished on us, his imperfect children.

The question is, do you know how great his affections are for you? Do you know you are loved by Almighty God himself—and not just loved as his creature, but as his child? For some of us, it's easier to believe that God, for some mysterious reason known only to himself, has saved us. But, if he were to be honest with us, he (barely) tolerates us at best. The pages of Scripture, however, tell us something far different, far more astonishing—that we have been adopted by God himself. Chosen. Cherished. Loved. Adored. I love the enthusiasm with which the apostle John proclaims this

---

2   David Crowder Band, John Mark McMillan. *How He Loves*. Studio album. sixstepsrecords. 2009.

truth: "See what great love the Father has lavished on us, that we should be called children of God! And that is what we are!" (1 John 3:1).

Children. Of. God. Unfathomable, but true.

Pastor and author Sinclair Ferguson says this truth—that God is our Father and we are his children—"lies at the heart of understanding the whole of the Christian life and all of the diverse elements in our daily experience. It is *the* way—not the *only* way, but the *fundamental* way—for the Christian to think about himself or herself. Our self-image, if it is to be biblical, will begin just here."[3] He is saying that when we think of God, the first thought that needs to come into our minds is *Father*. And when we think of ourselves, the first thing we need to think is *beloved child*. This foundation is the bedrock of our identity.

And, oh, doesn't your soul long for that—to know, and I mean really know, that you're loved with a love that is so steadfast, so safe, so pure, so good, and so abundant that you can rest deeply in it? A love that permeates your soul in such a way that, when you think of who you are, the first thing that comes to mind is *loved*?

But, if you're like me, your heart can simultaneously long for it yet refuse to believe it. For some, the idea of being God's beloved child feels more theoretical than actual, more wished-for than received. And in some ways, it's no wonder. We have three powerful enemies working hard to cause doubt and disbelief: the world, the flesh, and the Devil.

---

3   Sinclair B. Ferguson, *Children of the Living God* (Edinburgh: The Banner of Truth Trust, 2011), 2.

IDENTITY THEFT

The world increasingly communicates there's no such thing as a pure, abundant, and steadfast love of a Father for his child. Far too many fathers are absent, abusive, or just plain apathetic. Far too few children feel safe in their father's love. We see the ramifications of poor fatherhood all around us—in our cities, our neighborhoods, our homes, and even our own hearts. The wounds are deep, and the pain is real. The fallout of failed fatherhood produces hearts that find it hard to trust the love of a truly faithful and loving Father.

The world is broken; things are not the way they are supposed to be. I don't know your story, but I do know this: some of us have experienced the love of a good father, but many have not. And the nature of our relationship with our earthly father can greatly affect our ability to understand and trust the love of our heavenly Father. One thing we need to know is this—when God refers to himself as Father, he is referring to the kind of father we were created to have. Deep in our souls we know a father's love is meant to be life-giving. *His is.* A father's love is meant to be safe and pure. *His is.* A father's love should cause him to protect, provide, and be present. *His does.* Don't let the brokenness of the world eclipse your view of the love of a perfect Father.

The brokenness in the world is not the only thing creating this battle in our souls; our own flesh can work against us. We're prone to question *why* he loves us, *how* he can love us, and, ultimately, *if* he loves us. Like the younger brother in the parable of the prodigal son, we think, "I am no longer worthy to be called your [child]. Treat me as one of your hired servants" (Luke 15:19). We look at ourselves, knowing our sin, and think, *After all I have done, there is no way he could really love me.* But that's the point of the parable; don't look at yourself, look at the Father. His love is based on his character, not yours. His love is infinitely greater than all your sin.

Do you doubt such a love can exist? Do your circumstances make you wonder if the Father cares? Does your past tempt you to think you're unlovable or unworthy? Consider the truths in Ephesians 1:3–6:

> Blessed be the God and Father of our Lord Jesus Christ, who has blessed us in Christ with every spiritual blessing in the heavenly places, even as he chose us in him before the foundation of the world, that we should be holy and blameless before him. In love he predestined us for adoption to himself as sons through Jesus Christ, according to the purpose of his will, to the praise of his glorious grace, with which he has blessed us in the Beloved.

Do you hear it? He *chose* you out of his abundant love. He has *adopted* you. He has made you his own. And it brings him glory, praise, and joy. Let the truth of God's Word heal the wounds and replace the doubt and fear with the deep joy of an unfathomable and unfailing love.

Finally, the Devil, the enemy of our souls, delights in tempting us to doubt our true identity. His goal is to make you believe that you are still a slave, an orphan, or an illegitimate child—anything other than a beloved child of your Father.

The lie of the slave says you have to work, and work hard, to secure and sustain the Lord's love. Mess up and you're out; your worth is tied to your ability to produce and behave. The slave is always working, never resting.

The lie of the orphan says you've been abandoned and are all alone. No one really cares about you, provides for you, protects you, or loves you.

And the lie of the illegitimate child says you don't really belong, never did. The warmth and joy of family life is reserved for others—those who are more deserving, more talented, more favored, more anything.

Which of these lies plagues you the most? Has the world beaten you down in such a way that it hurts to even consider the love of a good Father? Does your flesh rise up and point out all of the reasons you could never be loved in this way? Does the enemy tempt you to think of yourself as a slave who can never do enough, an orphan who will never be wanted enough, or an illegitimate child who will simply never be enough?

IDENTITY TRUTH

The only antidote to the poison of these lies is the balm of the truth of Scripture. But, before we run to that healing balm, it's important to stop and clarify something. Is everyone a child of God? The answer is, no, not in the sense we're talking about. Every person is a *creation* of God, and he, as the Creator, certainly plays a fatherly role in many ways. But what we are talking about here is a special relationship that the New Testament uses two different terms to convey: new birth and adoption. They are two ways of looking at one reality—we have to *become* children of God.

The only way for this to happen is to be united, through faith, to the second person of the Trinity, the eternal Son of God. He was sent by the Father, took on human flesh, and came to rescue his siblings (Rom. 8:29). Paul tells us that "when the fullness of time had come, God sent forth his Son, born of woman, born under the law, to redeem those who were under the law, so that we might receive adoption as sons" (Gal. 4:4–5). John tells us, "But to all who did receive him (Jesus), who believed in his name, he gave the right to become children of God, who were born, not of blood nor of the will of the flesh nor of the will of man, but of God" (John 1:12–13). Adopted and born again. Children of God. If you've believed in Jesus through the work of the Spirit, then you can rest confidently in the truth of your identity—beloved child of the Almighty God.

This status is permanent and irreversible. Our adoption is a legal declaration on the part of God that involves his will and his Word and, therefore, cannot be undone. Our new birth is as irreversible as our physical birth. These are permanent acts of a sovereign God. So, the truth of our identity is unshakeable—but knowing, believing, and living in the truth can be hard.

On a personal level, our family's adoption story shaped my understanding of God's love in new ways. I know what it is to set my sights on a child not yet mine—and to pursue that child until she is. Our youngest was born in China, and the adoption process was difficult and costly. But that didn't matter; she was our daughter, and we would have done whatever it took to bring her home. So, we worked, we prayed, we cried, we filled out an inordinate amount of forms, we wrote checks, and we waited.

What was our sweet girl doing? Nothing! She was completely oblivious of all our efforts. Honestly, what could she have done? She couldn't initiate her own adoption process. She didn't peruse possible families and select ours. She didn't save her money and fund the adoption. The entire process rested on us and what we could and would do.

In the same way, we're unable to contribute to our adoption. We may like to think we chose God or merited our salvation in some way—but we didn't. Our adoption rests entirely on the will and the work of God. Similarly, we don't contribute to our new birth any more than my biological children contributed to theirs. As Ferguson says, "We can become his children only by the decision of God's will. The new birth . . . is not ours by nature, nor is it within our powers to accomplish!"[4]

So, child of God, rest. He has done it! He's gone to unimaginable extremes to make you his own. He's paid an extravagant price to call you his child. Consider Ephesians 1: "He chose us in him before the creation of the world to be holy and blameless in his sight. In love, he predestined us to be adopted as his sons through Jesus Christ, in accordance with his pleasure and will."

Think about that for a minute: *When* did he decide to love you? Before the creation of the world—before you did anything good or bad, he set his sights on you. *How* has he accomplished this adoption? Through the death of his true Son. And *why*? He wanted to (his will). It brings him joy (his pleasure). And he loves you (in love).

Let those truths sink in: He wanted you. He delights in you. He loves you.

IDENTITY TRANSFORMED

Oh, child of God, my prayer is that you and I would build our lives on this bedrock of truth. It's the foundation from which we live and move and have our being. God's love changes and transforms us. Children who live in the safety of their father's love delight to spend time with him, want to imitate him, and know how to rest securely because of his care. The love of our Father transforms us into children who do the same.

Like a child who can run to her father in any situation, so can we run to our heavenly Father. He cares about us in

---

4   Ferguson, *Children of the Living God*, 16.

every circumstance. When we're afraid, he's our strength (Isa. 12:2). When we're sad, he's our comfort (2 Cor. 1:3). When we're lonely, he's present (Ps. 46:1). When we're lost and confused, he's our way (Prov. 3:5–6). When we're anxious, he bears our burdens (1 Pet. 5:7). But we only know these things to be true as we spend time sitting with him, listening to him, and talking with him. Let his deep love for you lead you to spend time with him.

We also want to be like him. Have you ever seen a small child trying to shave like his father, push a lawn mower like his father, or wear her father's glasses? Naturally, children want to be like their father. They watch him, try to walk like him, talk like him, and act like him.

When God tells us to "be holy, for I am holy" (Lev. 11:44), he is inviting us to be like him. The Bible both tells us and shows us what God is like. And, when Jesus came, we saw exactly what God is like (John 14:9). We're called to imitate Jesus (1 Cor. 11:1) and be conformed to his image (Rom. 8:29). One day, we'll actually be like him (1 John 3:2)! The Father's love for us creates a new desire within us to be like him, more and more each day.

One of the sweetest blessings of living as a beloved child is to know deep rest. Have you seen a child quieted by the love of a tender parent? Frantic, worried, fearful, and angry cries are hushed as a child is held in the safe and tender arms of a parent. Zephaniah tells us we have a Father who not only "will rejoice over you with gladness," but also "will quiet you by his love" (Zeph. 3:17).

What causes you to be anxious and frantic? At the core of most of our strivings is a searching for worth. We all run to different things in the hopes of finding our value and meaning. We run to job titles, marital status, financial portfolios, the "success" of our children, friendships, applause, reputation, the cars we drive, and the neighborhoods we live in. But these things can neither confer nor confirm worth.

One of my favorite Christmas hymns says, "Long lay the world in sin and error pining, till he appeared and the soul felt its worth." Has your soul felt its worth? Only one thing can give your soul worth—to know you are a beloved child of God. This love dispels your doubts, fears, anxiety, worry, anger, and bitterness. In this love our strivings cease and we can rest.

Bask in the love of your Father. Delight in it; sing about it; remind yourself of it. Most of all, rest in it. He loves us. Oh, how he loves us.

VERSE TO MEMORIZE

In love he predestined us for adoption to himself as sons through Jesus Christ, according to the purpose of his will, to the praise of his glorious grace, with which he has blessed us in the Beloved.

Ephesians 1:4b–6

QUESTIONS FOR GROUP DISCUSSION

OPENING QUESTION: As you consider books you've read or TV shows you've watched, who's an example to you of an ideal father figure? What characteristics stand out to you?

1. How have you seen your relationship with your earthly father affect your understanding of your heavenly Father?

2. In what ways does someone live differently when she knows she is fully accepted and loved, not because of her efforts, but because she is someone's child?

3. READ ROMANS 8:14–17.

    a. How does a slave live differently than a son?

    b. How does this passage describe our relationship with God? How does believing this truth affect the way we live?

    c. What does it mean to be a fellow heir with Christ?

    d. As you consider your relationship with God, is it one of fear (like a slave) or one of family love and loyalty (like a son)? What would it look like to live as a beloved child of God?

4. READ I JOHN 3: 1–10.

    a. How does being a child of God affect our relationship with the world?

b. What is the relationship between obedience and being a child of God? Does our obedience transform us into a child of God, or does being a child of God transform us for obedience? How does the difference between those two affect how we live?

c. What does this passage tell us about those who make a practice of sinning? What is the difference between "continuing in a sin" and "fighting against sin"? Does this mean Christians never sin?

d. How can we recognize children of God?

5. Which lie from the Devil are you most tempted to believe: that you're a slave, an orphan, or an illegitimate child? How do each of these lies affect the way we live?

6. Consider Courtney's adoption story (or perhaps the adoption story of someone you know). How does adoption communicate and imitate the love of the Father for each of us?

7. When we believe we are truly a child of God, it transforms us in three ways: we delight to spend time with the Father, we want to imitate the Father, and we rest securely in the Father. Which of these do you struggle to do the most? Which one is most enjoyable for you? Why?

8. When someone knows she's loved, it affects every other part of her life. How does knowing the Father loves you allow you to love others in a Christ-like and sacrificial way?

9. As you think back over the chapter, what particular truth resonated with you? How will you live differently in light of that new understanding?

CHAPTER 4

SAINT: REDEEMED BY THE SON

MELISSA KRUGER

*According to the New Testament, saints are those
who belong to Christ, in whom Christ lives.
We are meant to be saints not only when we
get to heaven, but right here in this world.[1]*
—Elisabeth Elliot

I stare at the picture, looking at the woman smiling back at me. I immediately notice the imperfections: the shirt that doesn't hang quite right, the eyes marked by crow's feet, the uncooperative greying hair with the amazing ability to defy gravity, the extra weight hanging loosely on her entire frame. I see her, and I want to turn away. But I don't. I continue to

---

1   Elisabeth Elliot, *Be Still My Soul*, (Grand Rapids: Revell, 2003), 144

stare and pick apart all that is lacking. Who is this person I'm so tough on?

Myself.

And it's not just my physical appearance. I can easily list to you all the ways I'm lacking in more important areas. I haven't memorized books of the Bible or started a donation drive to help refugees. Some days I can barely get food on the table for my own family, much less invite the neighbors over for dinner. I haven't volunteered at my local pregnancy resource center or tutored kids in low income areas. My husband doesn't have hand-written notes packed in his lunch (what lunch?), and my children wore shorts to school (again) in 30-degree weather. I sinfully want my own way, and I grumble and complain when met by God with a different answer than "my will be done."

I'm overwhelmed by all that's missing. In my own estimation, I'm not a good enough friend, wife, mother, servant, co-worker, or Christian. There's a vast chasm between the me I am and the me I want to be.

Not enough. Failure. Sinner. These words imprint on my heart and impact my living.

Can you relate? Do you find yourself defined by failure or by sins that cling so close? What words do you wear comfortably as part of who you are? Angry. Promiscuous. Liar. Thief. Addict. Abortion. Pharisee. Failure. Anorexia. Discontent. Lustful. Lazy. Overweight. Unkind. Gossip. Not enough.

In some strange way, we become comfortable with these misplaced identities. They become part of who we are. We put them on like the stained and tattered old sweatshirt we've comfortably worn for years. We are the way we are, and there's really no hope of change.

Sometimes the pendulum swings, and I go a different route. In my attempt to rid myself of these ever-present accusations running around my mind, I work. I try harder. I pull myself up by my boot-straps, determined to do better. This striving usually lasts for about a day or two, maybe more if I'm really focused, and then I end up flat on my face, once again dealing with my inability to be the person I want to be.

I'm right back where I began: *Of course, I'm a sinner.*

It almost seems like a humble declaration, doesn't it? When I see myself as a sinner, I can stop trying so hard and expect everyone else to accept me just as I am.

IDENTITY THEFT

There's a reason I can live comfortably in the "I'm a sinner" identity: I am, in fact, still struggling with sin. The qualities I want to exhibit—love, joy, peace, patience, kindness, gentleness, goodness, faithfulness, and self-control—all too quickly succumb to grumbling, complaining, impatience, anger, and self-focus. Each day, I fail in a variety of ways.

Every false identity we adopt is rooted in some level of truth. The cleverest lies wrap falsehood with honesty. It's easy to succumb to discouragement and defeat.

Paul understood our struggle. He explained it to the Romans this way: "For I do not understand my own actions. For I do not do what I want, but I do the very thing I hate. . . . For I do not do the good I want, but the evil I do not want is what I keep on doing" (Rom. 7:15, 19).

Paul wrestled with sin. It warred within his soul:

> For I delight in the law of God, in my inner being, but I see in my members another law waging war against the law of my mind and making me captive to the law of sin that dwells in my members. Wretched man that I am! Who will deliver me from this body of death? (Rom. 7:22–24)

Paul's frustration with himself is apparent in this passage. He knows the person he wants to be—the person he should be—but he's aware of his shortcomings. His inward wrestling culminates in self-awareness of both his predicament and also his powerlessness.

And then, in a surprising twist, Paul is overcome with praise: "Thanks be to God through Jesus Christ our Lord!" (Rom. 7:25). Paul's self-understanding doesn't lead him to despair or discouragement. Yes, he knows his sin. But he knows something more important: there's a refuge for sinners.

All of the Old Testament foreshadows our need for rescue. Noah and his family escaped the flood by the ark. The Israelites escaped the destroying angel by the Passover lamb. Rahab escaped the destruction of Jericho by a scarlet cord. Time and again God provided a means to rescue his people. These mini-salvation stories all point to the ultimate rescuer: Jesus Christ.

Jesus is our ark of rescue, our Passover lamb of protection, our scarlet cord of security. All who are in Christ are safe. Why? Paul tells us in Romans 8:1–2, "There is therefore now no condemnation for those who are in Christ Jesus. For the law of the Spirit of life has set you free in Christ Jesus from the law of sin and death."

Satan shows us our sin so we might despair. He wants to steal, kill, and destroy. God shows us our sin to lead us to Jesus. He wants to give us life, and life to the full. We may struggle with sin, but it's no longer our identity if we're in Christ.

IDENTITY TRUTH

Scripture guides us to a right understanding of both God and ourselves. While it's true all have sinned and fallen short of the glory of God, once we come to Christ—once we're made new—that's no longer our name. Sin is no longer our defining quality.

What's our new name? It's surprising. It's unexpected. But it's true. We're no longer called sinners. We're called *saints*, which literally means, "holy ones."

Instinctively you might back away, exclaiming, "No way. I'm no saint and I'm certainly not holy. If you knew me and what I've done, you'd never use that term to describe me."

We often have a misguided notion that a saint is someone we eventually *become* after living a remarkable life. It's a title reserved for martyrs and monks, those whose lives are exemplary models of the Christian faith.

However, in Scripture, *saint* is never used that way. Paul writes time and again to the saints in various congregations: Rome, Corinth, Ephesus, Philippi, and Colossae. These believers weren't perfect. They believed wrong things about Jesus. They made sinful choices. Often Paul's letters corrected both unsound theology and erroneous living.

Yet he wrote to them as saints. Here's why. A saint isn't someone you become. It's who you are the moment you come to faith. God sets you apart, clothes you in the righteousness of Christ, and prepares good works for you to do. Every justified sinner is called a saint. Your identity is grounded in God's work in you, not your work for God. It's the name of all who cry out to God for mercy through Jesus Christ.

Sainthood isn't a measure of *our* works; it's a measure of Christ's works. Jesus resisted temptation. He obeyed God in everything. He lived a perfect life and gave it up so that he could be an atoning sacrifice. The just judgment of God for our sins was poured out on Jesus. In a sense, the cross acts as a sponge, soaking up the punishment we rightly deserve—Jesus takes every last drop. By his mercy, there's no punishment left for you or for me.

Not only does he wipe our slate clean, but we're also given the righteousness of Jesus. Paul explained, "For our sake he made him to be sin who knew no sin, so that in him we might become the righteousness of God" (2 Cor. 5:21). Our union with Christ envelopes us in his righteousness. It's a gift, freely given to all who believe.

This understanding is why we can rest with profound humility in our identity as a saint. We didn't earn it. We're not working toward it. We're saints not because of anything we've done, but because of who Jesus is. As Puritan pastor Thomas Brooks explains:

> God beholds his people in the face of his Son, and sees nothing amiss in them. He sees the sinner without spot or wrinkle. Christ makes us comely through his beauty. The Father honors us, delights in us, is well pleased with us, extends his love and favor to us, esteems us, and gives us free access to himself, in Christ. We are covered and hid under the precious robe of Christ's righteousness![2]

Say it to yourself. Declare this truth and extinguish the enemy's flaming darts. Daily rehearse it over and over:

I am a saint. I am a saint. I am a saint.

We may be uncomfortable with the label; we may want to protest our unworthiness; but that doesn't make our sainthood any less true. The more we understand our identity as a saint, the more we'll live in the freedom Christ offers. A new power attends our daily living, and we find his yoke easy, his burden light.

---

2   Thomas Brooks, *Works v:218-220 in Voices from the Past, Volume 2*, ed. Richard Rushing (Edinburgh, Scotland: Banner of Truth, 2016), 94.

IDENTITY TRANSFORMED

As saints, we live in the tension of "already, not yet." We've already been declared fully righteous, but we haven't yet been made fully righteous. As we deal with the residual effects of sin, we groan inwardly, awaiting the day when all is made right. Yet how we think about ourselves greatly affects how we live as we wait for Jesus to return.

Living as a saint who struggles with sin is profoundly different from living as a sinner who's desperately trying to be a saint.

It affects our daily lives in four ways.

First, when we understand our justification (that we've been declared righteous), we have a different relationship with sin. In our unbelief, sin was natural. We may have felt badly about certain things here or there, but we performed enough mental gymnastics to absolve ourselves of any need for true repentance.

As a saint, we're uncomfortable with sin. There's a fight going on within us. While we may conclude the battle waging in our hearts points to the fact we're sinners, it actually points to the fact we're saints. The Spirit awakens our heart to do battle. Outside of Christ, we're dead in our trespasses and sin—there's no sign of life. Unsaved sinners can't fight sin, because they're enslaved to it. Only saints, awakened by the Spirit, feel the battle Paul described.

Second, we live with hope in both our obedience and failure. Knowing all our good works are only done through the Spirit's power allows us to rejoice in our obedience. It's a sign of Christ's work in us! As Oswald Chambers notes, "The stamp of the saint is that he can waive his own rights and obey the Lord Jesus."[3]

No longer burdened with the law's demands, we can walk in the freedom of the Spirit's power. As the psalmist exclaims, "I run in the path of your commands, for you have set my heart free" (Ps. 119:32, NIV 1984). Our God-given new heart pumps spiritual life throughout our bodies so that we increasingly reflect the image of Jesus. A new hope awakens: to glorify God in all that we do.

When we disobey, we no longer hide. We mourn our sin and repent, knowing Jesus's blood is enough for all our failings. Saints approach the throne of grace with confidence instead of fear. We have a high priest who sympathizes with our weaknesses and offers mercy and help in our time of need. In both obedience and disobedience, we hope in the power of Jesus at work in us.

Third, our understanding of God's free grace allows us to live graciously toward others. We patiently and lovingly deal with the failings of others because we recognize the patience of our Savior toward us. Saints have no room for judgment of others because they recognize the truth in Paul's questions, "What do you have that you did not receive? If then you received it, why do you boast as if you did not receive it?" (1 Cor. 4:7). Saints humbly confront the wrong in others and point them to the fount of mercy and grace offered to all who believe. They are kind and tender, filled with hope in the Spirit's work as they live in true community with others.

Finally, saints are people of profound joy. They understand they've been rescued. Out of all the earth, they've been

---

3   Oswald Chambers, *My Utmost for His Highest* (Westwood, NJ: Dodd, Mead, & Company, 1935), 199.

called, saved, redeemed, and adopted into the family of God. Salvation—full, unmerited, free—is the bedrock of a saint's joy. As Isaiah prophesied:

> You will say in that day: "I will give thanks to you, O LORD, for though you were angry with me, your anger turned away, that you might comfort me. "Behold, God is my salvation; I will trust, and will not be afraid; for the LORD GOD is my strength and my song, and he has become my salvation." With joy you will draw water from the wells of salvation. (Isa. 12:1–3)

No matter what happens, whatever trials we face, whatever suffering we endure, our salvation is secure. The well of salvation offers refreshment on the most difficult of days. Christ holds us fast, and we rest secure in him.

Let me encourage you—as I need to encourage myself—to take your eyes off yourself. Stop replaying the scenes from the movie trailer of your life story that might be entitled, *I Am Not Enough*. Look upward. The cross is enough. Jesus is enough. His robes of righteousness cover you completely. Your identity is in him. Believe it, live in it, and rejoice today in this truth:

He calls you saint.

VERSE TO MEMORIZE

So then you are no longer strangers and aliens,
but you are fellow citizens with the saints
and members of the household of God.

Ephesians 2:19

QUESTIONS FOR GROUP DISCUSSION

OPENING QUESTION: When you hear the word "saint" what words or images usually come to mind?

1.   Do you resonate with feeling like you're "not enough"? How do we tend to focus on our imperfections? What areas can you pinpoint that we tend to struggle with feelings of failure?

2.   In what ways do we try in our own strength to measure up to others? How does this lead to both pride and despair?

3.   READ ROMANS 7:15–8:11.

   a.   Do you resonate with Paul's inner wrestling described in Romans 7:15–19? How have you seen this battle in your own life?

   b.   How does Paul describe himself? What does he desire? How does his struggle encourage you in your own faith?

   c.   What brings relief to Paul's inner wrestling? What is he thankful for?

   d.   How is it possible that "there is no condemnation for those in who are in Christ Jesus?" How does Christ free us from the law of sin and death?

   e.   Does this mean that Christians don't need to obey God? How would you answer that question in light of Romans 8:5–11?

f.   What does it mean that "he who raised Christ Jesus from the dead will also give life to your mortal
bodies?" How is that encouraging to you as you
fight against sin?

4.   READ ROMANS 1:7, I CORINTHIANS 1:2, EPHESIANS
1:1, PHILIPPIANS 1:1, AND COLOSSIANS 1:2. How do
these verses help you understand the term "saint"? How
is it similar to or different from your typical understanding of the word?

5.   Are you more comfortable thinking of yourself as
a sinner who is trying to be a saint or a saint who
still struggles with sin? Why does it matter how we
view ourselves?

6.   How does the fact that Christ makes us righteous (he
imputes his righteousness to us) affect how and why we
do good works?

7.   What role do our good works have as a saint? (See
Ephesians 2:10, 1 Peter 2:12, Colossians 1:8–10, Titus 3:8,
and Hebrews 10:24).

8.   How would living out your identity as a saint increase
your joy and peace?

9.   As you think back over the chapter, what particular
truth resonated with you? How will you live differently
in light of that new understanding?

CHAPTER 5

FRUITFUL:
FILLED WITH THE
HOLY SPIRIT

JASMINE HOLMES

*To enjoy God is the center of our rest and the
fountain of our blessedness and the chief end
for which we were made. It is our business to
seek him, and our happiness to enjoy him.*[1]
—Thomas Manton

"I'm kind of your typical perfectionist, Type A person," I
told my husband when we were dating.

Fast-forward to the conversation we had last year after
Phillip noticed my scatterbrained lack of organizational
skills, my laid-back approach to parenting, and my vehement

---

1   Thomas Manton, "By Faith" in *Voices from the Past*, Volume 2, ed.
     Richard Rushing (Edinburgh, Scotland: Banner of Truth, 2016), 214.

rejection of any attempt at scheduling. He pursed his lips one day and ventured, "Hey, babe . . . I don't think you're Type A after all."

It's true. I tend to thrive in organized chaos; in fact, too much organization makes me feel stifled and disingenuous (a real test for my real Type A husband). I've always been this way, ever since I was a little girl writing stories on the floor in my messy bedroom.

So why did I tell Phillip that I was Type A?

I said it because I struggle with anxiety and the pressure to perform. Rather than call anxiety what it was, I covered it with a label our culture pretends to loathe, but secretly loves: the control freak. She's the protagonist in just about every chick flick or drama, the locus of every stitch of advice we give to first-time moms, and the successful face we see on the cover of a magazine.

"I'm so Type A," she'll say, sighing and rolling her eyes heavenward. "I just need to learn to relax."

But we don't really want her to relax. We *love* the go-getter—she's part of the American dream.

So much so that this non-go-getter got a case of mistaken identity gazing upon her uptight and organizational beauty.

IDENTITY THEFT

Our culture is obsessed with *going, doing, being,* and *becoming.* Become the best version of yourself. Keep moving forward. Write your story.

Whether you're prone to jump on the hamster wheel and chase down the unattainable goal of perfection, or more like me (and find yourself lying down on the hamster wheel and being trampled by the more motivated hamsters) you've probably experienced the shame of not achieving all that you feel you ought.

There have been times when I've put my identity in my ability to achieve my goals, or in my lack thereof. Each of the different elements of my identity can be measured by the success I've achieved. As a wife, is my husband satisfied? As a mother, is my toddler keeping up with other children his age? As a teacher, are my students making amazing grades? As a woman, how am I stacking up in comparison to everyone else?

As a woman, the struggle takes on yet another dimension, because the teaching geared toward my sex often encourages me to find my identity in the doing. The Proverbs 31 woman becomes the standard, and my value is determined by my ability to measure up—by my ability to achieve, by my ability to *do*. I have often felt like my identity was measured by my ability to find a husband, keep him satisfied, bear him children, raise them well, and manage my home seamlessly.

And if I'm failing on one of those points, I'm worthless. Enter: shame.

I mean, consider this woman. She is more Type A than any Type A heroine who has ever graced the screen. She's buying property, sewing clothes, delegating tasks, taking care of her servants . . . and I'm writing this chapter at 10:51 a.m., and I haven't even gotten dressed yet.

However, as author Wendy Alsup explains, the Proverbs 31 woman isn't a daily standard we must seek to fulfill:

> We need to understand how to read and apply this genre in order to fully appreciate and understand Proverbs 31. This will free us from the misguided way this

chapter is sometimes used to demoralize women with often unattainable standards.[2]

Proverbs is a book of wisdom, which we generally understand—until we get to that last chapter.

Take, for example, Proverbs 26:4: "Answer not a fool according to his folly, lest you be like him yourself." And Proverbs 26:5: "Answer a fool according to his folly, Or he will become wise in his own eyes."

We know God doesn't contradict himself. We understand that, sometimes, it's fruitful to answer a fool, while others, it isn't. Wisdom dictates the difference.

Proverbs 31:10–31 is probably not a day in the life of a godly woman. It's an intricate tableau of different facets of excellence. It's not a point-by-point guide to wifehood, but a picture of obedience expressed in all different aspects and seasons of life. It's superhuman; probably because it's not a picture of a specific woman, but a passage meant to draw us into deeper reliance on Christ as we strive to be faithful in all of our duties at home and abroad.

Alsup continues:

> You cannot read Proverbs the same way you read the Ten Commandments, yet many Christians fear situational wisdom. Some don't trust others to figure out what applies and how to apply it, so they enforce one-dimensional conclusions that don't allow for the nuances that much of the biblical proverbs offer. The

2   Wendy Alsup, *Is the Bible Good for Women* (New York: Multnomah, 2017), 53.

answer to such fear is to apply wisdom in ways that are actually wise through the indwelling of the Holy Spirit.[3]

God will tell us when to rest. He will tell us when to strive. Wisdom to discern what is best is where the abiding comes in.

IDENTITY TRUTH

If our identity can't be found in the Type A go-getter who's chasing the American dream or in her sanctified Proverbs 31 counterpart, where are we supposed to look?

John 15:1–5 comes forward to give us the answer:

> I am the true vine, and my Father is the vinedresser. Every branch in me that does not bear fruit he takes away, and every branch that does bear fruit he prunes, so that it may bear more fruit. Already you are clean because of the word that I have spoken to you. Abide in me, and I in you. As the branch cannot bear fruit by itself, unless it abides in the vine, neither can you, unless you abide in me. I am the vine; you are the branches. Whoever abides in me and I in him, he it is that bears much fruit, for apart from me you can do nothing.

During intimate moments with his disciples, Jesus paused to remind them of the place true fruitfulness can be found: in him.

A few verses before, he promised the Holy Spirit, saying, "And I will ask the Father, and he will give you another Helper, to be with you forever, even the Spirit of truth, whom

---

3   Ibid.

the world cannot receive, because it neither sees him nor knows him. You know him, for he dwells with you and will be in you" (John 5:16–17).

Paul pressed deeper into the benefits of the indwelling power of the Holy Spirit and our connection to the mind of God in 1 Corinthians 2:6–16, reminding us that "the Spirit searches everything, even the depths of God" (1 Cor. 2:10) and that, by his power, we are enabled to understand the things "freely given to us by God" (1 Cor. 2:12).

By the power of Christ's atoning death on the cross, we abide with the God of the universe, and through that relationship, we bear fruit—part of which is a deeper understanding of what he desires from us.

We can run around like chickens with our heads cut off all we want. And so often, we do just that—trying to achieve and succeed in our own power, and for our own glory. But the Scriptures remind us again and again that true fruitfulness is found only by abiding in Christ.

True fruitfulness is found in rest.

We want so badly to focus on the come and do, but the true message of the gospel bids us to come and die.

IDENTITY TRANSFORMED

I want to be careful here, because the doing is not divorced from the dying. But the dying comes first.

As Paul boldly proclaimed: "Therefore, if anyone is in Christ, he is a new creation. The old has passed away; behold, the new has come" (2 Cor. 5:17). And again: "I have been crucified with Christ. It is no longer I who live, but Christ who lives in me. And the life I now live in the flesh I live by faith in the Son of God, who loved me and gave himself for me" (Gal. 2:20).

Faith without works is dead (James 2:17). But before we can begin to do the work of faith, we must die the death it requires of us. We can't run straight to the work without first placing our faith and our identity in Christ. There is *doing* in our new identity, but it is anchored in the fact that we are *becoming* more like Christ as we continue to abide in him.

Abiding in Christ is not a passive activity. Jesus commanded us to abide in him and reminded us that we cannot bear fruit apart from him. Sinclair Ferguson reminds us of four truths about abiding in Christ:

> FIRST, union with our Lord depends on his grace. Of course we are actively and personally united to Christ by faith (John 14:12). But faith itself is rooted in the activity of God.

> SECOND, union with Christ means being obedient to him. Abiding involves our response to the teaching of Jesus: "If you abide in me, and my words abide in you . . ." (John 15:7a).

> THIRD, Christ underlines a further principle, "Abide in my love" (15:9), and states very clearly what this implies: the believer rests his or her life on the love of Christ.

> FINALLY, we are called, as part of the abiding process, to submit to the pruning knife of God in the providences by which he cuts away all disloyalty and sometimes all

that is unimportant, in order that we might remain in Christ all the more wholeheartedly.[4]

I love this explanation. By depending on Christ's grace, we're able to obey his commands, rest in his love whether we fail or succeed, and submit to his will as he makes us more like him.

So, the doing is important; but to focus on the doing without the abiding centers our efforts on the sheer force of our own will rather than becoming more like Christ by submitting to his will. All the activity in the world is fruitless if we're not abiding in the vine. What we produce from that straining is about as satisfying as a mouthful of dust.

If we're marching down the to-do list and chasing after a cultural perception of success, we will always come up empty. The things of this earth were not meant to satisfy us. Our true treasures are stored in heaven (Matt. 6:19–20). Even if we're striving toward good and biblical things—but doing so divorced from the love and wisdom found through abiding in Christ—we are ultimately striving after wind (Eccles. 1:14).

This is not the Type B girl trying to tell you to settle down and stop working. On the contrary, whatever personality type we possess, the Spirit is in the business of conforming us to the image of Christ (Rom. 8:29). There is a ditch on both sides of the road, from fruitless striving to slothful complacency (Prov. 19:25).

I do think we're more sensitive toward laziness and lack of effort than we are toward go-getting and lack of rest in Christ. However, neither of those meets the goal of union with Christ: abiding in him and following him as he guides

---

4   Sinclair Ferguson, "What Does It Mean To Abide In Christ?" Ligonier Ministries, February 19, 2018, https://www.ligonier.org/blog/what-does-it-mean-abide-christ/.

our steps, giving us wisdom in how best to pursue him in our daily lives.

Are you abiding in Christ, or are you abiding in the security of the work of your hands? Are you abiding in Christ, or are you walking in shame at the *lack* of the work of your hands? Neither will do. And neither is what we are called to.

Our identity is found in abiding in Christ. If we're fruitful, it's because he has given us increase, and we praise him for that. If we're floundering, we rest in the fact that our true worth comes from his work on our behalf, and we praise him for that.

In either season, we press toward the mark, resting and working for his glory alone. That is where our identity lies.

VERSE TO MEMORIZE

I am the vine; you are the branches. Whoever abides in me and I in him, he it is that bears much fruit, for apart from me you can do nothing.

John 15:5

QUESTIONS FOR GROUP DISCUSSION

OPENING QUESTION: As you consider our culture, how do you observe the pursuit to do more, be more, know more, and produce more?

1. In what ways do we place our identity in our achievements? How do we seek significance in what we do?

2. How does constantly trying to measure up lead to exhaustion? In what area of your life today do you feel like you'll never be enough?

3. How can a life of striving by our own efforts (rather than abiding in Christ) lead us to both judgement of others and despair in our own life?

4. READ JOHN 15:1–11.

   a. According to this passage what does it mean to abide in Jesus?

   b. When we fail to abide in Jesus, what happens? What do you think it looks like when we attempt to do work for Jesus without abiding in him?

   c. How does time with Jesus nourish our soul in a similar way that food and water nourish our body?

   d. According to verse 11, why does Jesus want us to abide in him? What is he hoping for in your life, and how does that help you as you think about abiding with him?

5. Often, we tell ourselves we are too busy to spend time reading the Bible or in prayer. What practical ways can we fight against this tendency? What has helped you carve out time for abiding in the midst of a busy life of doing?

6. READ PROVERBS 31:10–31.

    a. How does understanding the Proverbs 31 woman as an example to learn from rather than a standard to compare yourself to give you encouragement?

    b. In the midst of all her activity, verse 30 guides us to what fuels her efforts. How does abiding in Jesus lead us to a life of fruitfulness?

    c. One thing that always strikes me about the Proverbs 31 woman is her laughter. In the midst of her busy life, she is a woman of joy. In contrast, how does busyness apart from Jesus lead us to weary work and exhausting effort?

7. READ GALATIANS 5:22-23. How does this verse shape your understanding of Spirit-filled fruitfulness? How is this type of fruitfulness different than what you usually think of in terms of achievement or success?

8. Consider each of these nine aspects of fruitfulness from Galatians 5:22-23. Which of these do you struggle with the most in the midst of the busyness of doing?

9. As you think back over the chapter, what particular truth resonated with you? How will you live differently in light of that new understanding?

CHAPTER 6

MEMBER: CONNECTED TO THE CHURCH

MEGAN HILL

The spiritual fellowship that a believer enjoys with his Redeemer, is not a solitary or selfish joy, but one which he cannot possess alone, or except in common with other believers.[1]
—James Bannerman

After Hurricane Katrina passed through my state in 2005, I was selected to be a research subject for a study conducted by Harvard Medical School. At regular intervals following

---

1   James Bannerman, *The Church of Christ: A Treatise on the Nature, Powers, Ordinances, Discipline and Government of the Christian Church*, vol. 1 (1868; repr. Birmingham, AL: Solid Ground Christian Books, 2009), 19.

the storm, researchers from Harvard called to ask me a set of questions about my mental and emotional health, as well as questions about my social support system. Each time, the caller asked: "How many people in your community would you be comfortable asking to borrow a cup of sugar?" I would do some quick mental math: "Let's see. About 100?" That question was always immediately followed by: "How many people in your community would you be comfortable sharing your thoughts and feelings with?" I would answer: "The same."

Though the researchers had never met me, my answer to those two questions was an important clue to my identity. The reason I had such a sizable collection of sugar-lending, feelings-sharing friends was because I belonged to a local church. The truth is, never once—in storm or sunshine— have I been alone in the world. And no Christian ever has.

So far in this book, we've considered several aspects of what it means for a Christian to find her identity in Christ. Now, we will turn our attention to the precious truth that belonging to Christ means we also belong to everyone else who belongs to him. In Christ, we are not simply individuals; we are joined to what Peter calls a "chosen race, a royal priesthood, a holy nation" (1 Pet. 2:9). In Christ, we are part of the church.

IDENTITY THEFT

To say that my identity is necessarily connected to the people in my church is hardly popular in our present culture. Our unbelieving friends and neighbors—and, sadly, even many of those who profess faith—reject the importance of membership in a local church. Most likely, we've been influenced by that lie ourselves. To reorient ourselves, let's begin by unmasking four common ways our identity as part of Christ's church may have been stolen:

Theft #1: My relationship to God is personal.

Like most seductive untruths, this one has a kernel of truth in it. Each one of us must repent of sins and trust in Christ (Mark 1:15). Each of us ought to study God's Word and pray in private (Ps. 119:11, Matt. 6:6). Each one should rejoice in the precious fact that her name is written in heaven (Luke 10:20). Our relationship to God *is* personal. But we lose our identity when we believe our relationship to God is *only* personal.

This untruth is pervasive. Sociologist Christian Smith studied the religious lives of American teens and young adults and found people think "each individual is uniquely distinct from all others and deserves a faith that fits his or her singular self . . . [and] that religion need not be practiced in and by a community."[2] To many people, faith is so personal it can't be shared or even discussed with others, and any type of "organized religion" is contrary to authentic spiritual experience.

Even if you haven't swallowed the lie in these blatant forms, you may have thought something like, *I just feel closer to God when I'm alone out on the beach or hiking in the woods. I don't have that same experience in church.* But anytime we believe our spiritual condition is better—more authentic, more fruitful, more profound—apart from the church, we've allowed our identity as members of the church to be stolen.

---

2   Christian Smith, *Soul Searching: The Religious and Spiritual Lives of American Teenagers* (Oxford, UK: Oxford University Press, 2005), 147.

Theft #2: My personality isn't suited to church.

You don't have to spend much time on social media before someone will invite you to take a personality test. These assessments—whether well-regarded scientific tools or silly quizzes based on movie characters—purport to reveal truths about who you really are. For example, a personality indicator may tell you that you're an extrovert (someone who thrives in the company of others) or an introvert (someone who works best alone). It may tell you that you learn by doing things, rather than being told about them. It may suggest you flourish when you act according to your own intuition, rather than by making rational conclusions based on information.

Personality tests can have value—the silly quizzes give us a chance to laugh, and the psychological tools may help us to pinpoint our natural weaknesses and strengths—but they can never define who we are. Whether your personality tends to be introverted or extroverted, sensory or intuitive, rational or emotional or anything else, only God can authoritatively declare who you are and what you need to be truly happy. So if you have ever allowed yourself to think, *I'm an introvert; church is not the place where I do best*, your identity has been stolen.

Theft #3: I'm already part of a community of people with whom I have a lot in common.

For everyone who believes she is better off alone, there are still plenty of people who value community. We have communities in our towns: photography clubs, book groups, parent-teacher organizations. We have communities online: Facebook groups for women in ministry and discussion boards for special-needs moms. We have communities at work and school: people with whom we play softball or eat

lunch or write poetry. We form communities with our neighbors, our friends from college, and our fellow bird-watchers.
We even belong to communities with spiritual purposes: Bible studies, accountability groups, women's shelter volunteers.

In these communities we can be encouraged and helped
by other people who share the same interests and circumstances. But we get into trouble if we believe our most
important relationships are with the people we've selected
for ourselves. Unlike our self-chosen communities, the local
church is a community of people God has chosen for us, for
his glory and our good. If you tend to think, *No one at church
gets me like the people at my gym do,* you've believed a lie. Those
other communities might be naturally comfortable, but
they're not where your ultimate identity lies.

Theft #4: I'm focusing on my family.

Each of us has a community clearly given to us by God: our
family. Whether your family consists of parents, siblings,
husband, or kids, you have certain people whose lives are
permanently linked to yours. And God has given you specific commands to govern your relationship. You are called to
honor your parents (Ex. 20:12), respect your husband (Eph.
5:33), and graciously care for your children (Eph. 6:4).

It's good to be a part of a natural family and to diligently care for them as God has commanded. We *are* daughters,
mothers, wives, and sisters. But even these important roles
do not eclipse our identity in the eternal family of God. As
Christian women, we are the children of God (Gal. 4:6),
mothers and sisters to the fellow-members of our local
church (1 Tim. 5:2, see also Titus 2:3–5), and part of Christ's
beloved bride (Rev. 21:9). If ever you say to yourself, *I'm the
mom of three young kids! I'll get back to church in a few years,*
you've had your identity stolen.

IDENTITY TRUTH

Now that we've uncovered some of the fake IDs that we may have tucked in our wallets, it's time to search the Bible to find out what our true identity is. We will see it's the clear testimony of Scripture that a Christian is a member of Christ's church.

We don't have to read too far into the Bible—in fact, depending on your Bible, it might even be on the first page—to learn that God made people to be together. On the sixth day of the world, God made a man. But he didn't stop at making just one human. He made a companion for him (Gen. 2:7, 18, 22). We might first think these verses are about marriage, and that's true. But this isn't just a text about marriage. It's a text about the church.[3] When God put Adam and Eve together in the garden, he established the first church. Adam and Eve worked and worshiped together, and it was very good.

Of course, just a few verses later, Adam and Eve fell into sin (Gen. 3:6–7). The perfect relationship they had with one another and with God became tarnished and broken. Anyone who has spent time in the local church can testify that sin still complicates nearly everything we do together.

But, as we continue in the Scriptures, we see that God did not abandon his imperfect church. Adam's family-church continued and grew across the generations: Seth, Noah, Abraham, Isaac, Jacob. The worshipers of God were not solitary individuals; they were members of a family with whom God established a relationship. God brought Abraham to Canaan, not as one man, but as the father of a family

---

3　Christopher Ash, *Marriage: Sex in the Service of God* (Vancouver, British Columbia: Regent College Publishing, 2003), 119-122.

who would worship him. God redeemed the Israelites from Egypt, not one by one, but as a gathered people. God sent Moses and the prophets to proclaim his Word, not primarily to individuals, but to his people together. When we think of Israel in the Old Testament, even with all its clearly-visible faults, we ought to recognize it as the church.

In the fullness of time, we come to the advent of Christ. God was made man for our sake—he entered into our human condition, bore the curse of our sin on the cross, and rose again as the first fruit of our own new life. The glorious purpose of Christ's incarnation, obedience, death, and resurrection was so that he might "present the church to himself in splendor, without spot or wrinkle or any such thing, that she might be holy and without blemish" (Eph. 5:27). Christ came to make us part of his church.

Moving further into the New Testament, we see this theme continues. Whenever people came to Christ in faith, they also became part of the church. Consider this description of the believers in the book of Acts: "And they devoted themselves to the apostles' teaching and the fellowship, to the breaking of bread and the prayers. . . . And the Lord added to their number day by day those who were being saved" (2:42, 47). The church gathers; people are saved; they join the church. There are no lone Christians in the New Testament.

The New Testament Epistles—letters written to the early believers—reinforce this identity truth. The church is called a plant (Rom. 11:17–24, cf. John 15:1–7), a building (Eph. 2:18–22), and a body (Rom. 12:4–5; 1 Cor. 12:12–27; Eph. 4:15–16). Each of these images emphasizes the fact that our connection to Christ necessarily connects us to everyone else connected to him. We are the tendrils that draw their common life from Christ the central vine. We are the bricks that together rest on Christ the foundation. We are the hands and feet and eyes and ears of Christ who is the head.

Just as being a member of the church is our present identity, we also see in Scripture that it will be our future identity. The book of Revelation draws back the curtain on eternity and allows us to see the reality of things to come. There we read, "And I [John] saw the holy city, new Jerusalem, coming down out of heaven from God, prepared as a bride adorned for her husband. And I heard a loud voice from the throne saying, 'Behold the dwelling place of God is with man. He will dwell with them, and they will be his people, and God himself will be with them as their God'" (Rev. 21:2–3). God's people always have been part of the church, and God's people always will be part of the church.

The church is not a human invention—a group of people who thought it would be a good idea to get together since they share the same beliefs and spiritual practices. The church is established by Christ, protected and nourished by Christ, governed by Christ, and exists for the glory of Christ. Because of this, the church is also not optional—a group that you could join or not join, depending on your personality and preferences. The church is fundamental to the identity of everyone who belongs to Christ.

IDENTITY TRANSFORMED

So what does it mean that our identity is permanently—eternally!—linked to the church? We have seen from Scripture that if you are a Christian, you are united to God's people. And being connected to the church is one of the greatest blessings we experience. Let's consider four practical ways that we live out our identity as members of Christ's church:

Join a local church.

We can't be a part of Christ's church in the abstract. Owning our identity will mean we choose an actual, biblical congregation of believers near the place where we live. We don't pick a church based on our personality and preferences, of course. The important thing here is to find a church that's committed to a biblical statement of faith, preaches and teaches the Word of God, and is organized under biblical leadership.[4]

Then, having found a good local church, we publicly align with it. We meet with the elders, give our Christian testimony, and stand up front to take the membership vows. In short, we join the church.

As members of the church, we receive all the blessings that Christ bestows. In the church, we come under the spiritual care of the church's leaders. In the church, we join a community of people invested in each other's welfare—people who share their cups of sugar and listen to one another's thoughts and feelings. In the church, we work and worship alongside people who are mutually committed to the One whom our own souls love best. In the church, we fully live out our identity.

Submit to the leaders of your church.

Ultimately, the church is under the leadership of Christ who is her head. And the risen and ascended Christ has given a gift to the church in this world: pastors and teachers (Eph.

---

4 For more about choosing a local church, see: "What Should I Look for in a Church?," 9Marks, https://www.9marks.org/answer/what-should-i-look-church/.

4:8–11). Our life of faith is not a self-directed journey; we walk in the paths Christ has marked, submitting to the leadership of the men he has placed in authority. As Hebrews 13:17 tells us, "Obey your leaders and submit to them, for they are keeping watch over your souls, as those who will have to give an account. Let them do this with joy and not with groaning, for that would be of no advantage to you."

This means we gladly receive the Word when they preach and teach it to us. It means we seek to put those sermons into practice. It means we turn to them for biblical counsel and commit ourselves to implementing their vision for the church. Under the authority of godly leadership, our souls receive the tender ministry of Christ himself (1 Thess. 2:13).

Pray for your church.

Because Christ builds his church and protects his church (Matt. 16:18), Christ is the one to whom we should bring the church's needs. And perhaps nothing will help us to love our church more than prayer. By God's design, the church is filled with a diverse group of people who don't always share our personality, or interests, or stage of life. In other circumstances, we might never choose to be friends with any of them. And yet God has called us to love one another. In prayer, we have an opportunity to "rejoice with those who rejoice" and "weep with those who weep" (Rom. 12:15). In prayer, the members of the church "bear one another's burdens" (Gal. 6:2). In prayer, we invest ourselves in the good of those who share our identity.

Support your church in her worship and work.

Because our identity is tied to the church, we live out our identity by participating in the church for the good of the church and the glory of Christ her Lord. At the most basic level, this means we will be present when the church gathers. When God's people are meeting together to worship him, we're there—adding our voices to the praise, joining our hearts to the prayer, and submitting to the Word alongside everyone else who shares our common identity.

What's more, the Lord has given each of us gifts—not to serve our own aims, but for "the common good" (1 Cor. 12:7). Before we were even born, God prepared specific opportunities for us to use those gifts to serve his body (Eph. 2:10). This means we will assist the church's work however we can. We greet visitors, make phone calls, knock on doors, practice hospitality, assemble casseroles, hold babies, organize Bible studies, visit widows, welcome strangers, and disciple younger women. We will also have the blessing of receiving ministry from others. In the church, we will be greeted, welcomed, served, taught, and prayed for by others who are using their own gifts. In all the various tasks of the church, we each live out our identity.

Though the world would tell us that church is an option, an irrelevance, or even an obstacle, we know better. Our identity is eternally connected to the people of God. We are each a vital part of the church, and the church is essential to who we are.

VERSE TO MEMORIZE

But as it is, God arranged the members in the body, each one of them, as he chose.

1 Corinthians 12:18

QUESTIONS FOR GROUP DISCUSSION

OPENING QUESTION: Did you grow up as a member of a church? If you did, was your family an "Easter and Christmas" type family, a "we were there every time the doors were open" type of family, or somewhere in between?

1. Why do we often think of faith as personal and private?

2. Which of the four types of identity theft discussed in the chapter is most common in your community or perhaps in your own life?

3. READ ACTS 2:42–47.

   a. What various aspects of life in the early church are described in this passage?

   b. How is this description similar to or different from the church you attend?

4. How have you experienced the blessing of being part of a church? Why at times can it also be difficult to be a member of a church?

5. READ I CORINTHIANS 12:12–26 AND RO-
   MANS 12:3–13.

   a. What do both these passages teach about the body of Christ?

   b. In what ways does being a part of the church allow us to both experience and express the love of Christ?

c. Have you ever felt unneeded in the church or that your service isn't important? What truths from 1 Corinthians 12 can help you fight against that false belief?

d. What are the variety of ways Romans 12:3–13 shows us we can serve in the church?

e. According to this passage, in what ways is humility required of each member of the church?

6. Why is prayer such an important part of life together in the church? Consider the letters of Paul. We often hear of his prayers for the church. How does prayer build up the church?

7. READ EPHESIANS 4:11–16.

a. What is the role of shepherds and teachers in the church?

b. Why are we likely to be carried away by false teaching if we aren't connected to a local church?

c. What happens if one part of your physical body isn't working properly? How does that affect the rest of your body? How do you think this principle applies in the life of the church?

8. The chapter discussed four ways we can live out our identity in the church. In which of these ways do you want to grow in your participation in the life of the church?

9. As you think back over the chapter, what particular truth resonated with you? How will you live differently in light of that new understanding?

CHAPTER 7

BEAUTIFUL: CLOTHED IN SPLENDOR

TRILLIA NEWBELL

> *Our efforts at beauty—whether in art, music, homemaking, or anything else—can serve similar purposes in nourishing our souls, in encouraging and blessing others, and in honoring the beautiful and beauty-making Creator.*[1]
> —Joe Rigney

Five o'clock in the morning comes early. For Tish, a mother of three, it felt as if a two-by-four had been placed on her forehead, pushing her back down into her soft feather pillow. Yet when the alarm rang, she resisted the urge to stay in bed. She slowly rolled over and placed one foot on the floor, then

---

[1] Joe Rigney, *The Things of Earth* (Wheaton: Crossway, 2015), 212.

another, struggling to find her workout clothes in the dark. She knew if she didn't do it *now* it would never get done. So Tish headed to the living room, eyes half shut, and began her routine: read the Word, pray, do a 30-minute workout.

The workout was a new part of her daily routine, part of a weight-loss goal she set for herself. And though adding those 30 minutes to the beginning of her busy day was far from easy, she was determined.

Week one went by—smooth sailing. Week two came and went, and she finally began to feel like she had a solid routine. But by week three, the scale began to get the best of her. She started to feel discouraged because, though her energy and stamina were increasing, her weight had only *slightly* changed. After all that work!

Frustrated and discouraged, Tish began to think of alternatives. She thought about a popular new diet she heard about from a friend that guaranteed a loss of ten pounds in one week. She tried it and lost some weight, but not quite the promised ten pounds. Eventually her enthusiasm waned, and the diet's restrictions started to feel like too much. Soon she was off the diet and had quickly gained all the weight back.

Frustrated once again, Tish decided to take a different approach. She went to a trusted friend for help.

"Are you doing this to be healthy or because you want to be skinny?" her friend asked.

Tish knew she had to answer honestly. "I want to be skinny."

Her friend gently said, "Perhaps that's the problem. If you go about this with a desire to be healthy and glorify the Lord with your body, you will be satisfied. Not necessarily satisfied in yourself or how you look, but satisfied in God."

IDENTITY THEFT

Many of us can relate to Tish's story. Maybe it's not the scale that gets you. Perhaps it's the way your hair falls or how your eyes fit in on your face or your lack of curves. Whatever it is, our focus on physical appearance can be all-consuming and crushing. Magazine covers give us a picture of the ideal woman that can only truly be achieved through Photoshop. And then there are all the quick-fix "solutions" found in bookstores and on the internet. Television and movies proclaim that beauty is defined by our outward appearance. But it's not just cultural influences that affect our focus on outward appearance.

Before I knew magazines existed—or at least that they often featured female beauties on their covers—I would look in the mirror with a hint of disgust and misery. My nose appeared large and in charge of my face. I hated it. I thought I was ugly. I can't remember the age when I started becoming more aware of my appearance, but I do know it was well ahead of my teen years. There was something in my heart that drove me to be dissatisfied with the way the Lord had created me. I didn't have the words or the maturity to analyze it then. But now as I reflect on that wrestling and discontentment, I know that my trouble wasn't outward, but inward.

Even at that young age, I had internalized three common lies about beauty that can steal away joy and identity in the area of beauty and lead us into sin and misery. Each of them is related to a sin that is so easy for us to fall for:

- "Outward appearance is all important!" (idolatry)
- "I must measure up!" (envy, greed, and pride)
- "I have to be beautiful to be acceptable or desirable!" (fearing other people)

Lie #1: Appearance Is Queen

We typically look in the mirror at least once a day—some of us far more often. We may step on the scale, scrutinize our every pound, or keep trying on those jeans that we only wish we could still fit into. What are we longing for when we're discouraged by our outward appearance? Could it be that, like our culture in general, we've misplaced the significance of beauty and made it a god?

I've heard it said that idolatry makes good things into god things and therefore into bad things. Beauty, as we will soon see, is a good thing. And a desire to be beautiful isn't in itself sinful—not until we take beauty and make it an idol.

In the time before Christ, people didn't hide their idols. They were visible and plain to see. The prophet Isaiah poked fun at idols when compared to the real God:

> To whom then will you liken God, or what likeness compare with him? An idol! A craftsman casts it, and a goldsmith overlays it with gold and casts for it silver chains. He who is too impoverished for an offering chooses wood that will not rot; he seeks out a skillful craftsman to set up an idol that will not move. (Isa. 40:18–20)

Can you imagine what our idols might look like today? We can turn *anything* into an idol, and we are skilled at masking our idols. We can even excuse them away as something like preference. But the heart of idolatry is forgetting who God is and worshiping self instead.

Our idolatry of beauty can lead to emotional responses regarding our appearance. Some diagnostic questions to consider: How do you respond when you can't fit into that old dress, and how long does the failure affect you? Do you struggle with intimacy with your spouse as a result of how you feel about your body? Are you abusing food or your body in any way in an effort to be "skinny"?[2] Do you agonize over your looks, constantly seeking to alter or augment something in order to feel better about yourself? Are you ever content? How about your financial investment; would it reveal where your heart is (Matt. 6:21)?

Idolatry takes something potentially good and makes it too important. That means some of the things we idolize—even beauty and external appearance—can be good and healthy in themselves. But when they take over our hearts and minds, they quickly fill the space only God is supposed to occupy.

Lie #2: If I Only Looked Like Her

I remember not wanting to go to the gym after having my first child. It wasn't that I didn't enjoy exercise or that I had no motivation to work out. What bothered me was the prospect of exercising beside women who were in better shape. I was embarrassed by how I looked and by my inability to walk up a flight of stairs without stopping. I realize now just how misguided these thoughts and feelings were, but they were real—and difficult to handle.

I was learning firsthand the pitfalls of *comparison*.

It's probably impossible to avoid a certain level of comparison with others. And some comparison can be harmless or even helpful, prompting us to better ourselves and even to enjoy the beauty of God's diverse creation. But comparing ourselves to others so easily becomes harmful to ourselves,

---

2   If you have been diagnosed or suspect that you might struggle with an eating disorder, please seek professional help.

to others, and to our relationship with God. In other words, comparison easily becomes sinful.

Sinful comparison snuffs out trust and gratitude. It steals joy and makes it difficult to love our neighbors. (I was so focused on myself, for example, that I missed out on opportunities to get to know other women in the gym.) It creates envy, greed, and competitiveness, which can lead to other problems. "For where jealousy and selfish ambition exist, there will be disorder and every vile practice" (James 3:16).

Does it sound strange to state that sinful comparison is essentially pride? It's true. Pride in the biblical sense is essentially egotism or a misplaced sense of self-worth. That misplaced sense of self compels us to compare ourselves to others, either negatively or positively, and that in turn disturbs our relationships with God and others. No wonder the apostle Paul instructed us, "Do nothing from selfish ambition or conceit, but in humility count others more significant than yourselves" (Phil. 2:3).

How do we kill pride and fight our tendency toward comparison? The short answer is found in Paul's statement: we must pursue humility. We will look more closely at how to do that below.

Lie #3: Beauty Equals Acceptance

The final lie involves what others think about us—or what we think about what others think. This lie tells us that if we're not beautiful by worldly standards, then we won't be accepted or desired. Not surprisingly, this lie leads us to place too much value on the opinions of others and spend too much energy worrying about how they might view us.

It's true, of course, that some people who live by worldly standards do judge others by appearance and reject those who don't measure up. But worldly standards are not true standards! When we forget that bedrock reality, we fall into what the Bible calls the "fear of man"—or the fear of other people.

This fear is known in Scripture as a snare (Prov. 29:25). A snare is a trapping device that often consists of a noose. I picture a wild animal being captured by hunters. Once the animal is caught with that loop of rope or twine, it has no chance. That's what fear of other people does. It can trap you. It can choke the life out of you. Or it can lead you to do things you wouldn't normally do.

When we're struggling with the fear of acceptance, we worry a lot about how we look to others. For some, this fear can be debilitating, and it can lead to painful results. A woman who fears that her husband doesn't find her attractive could end up desiring the attention of another man or even having an affair. Someone insecure about her looks could spend a fortune in beauty treatments or flood her social media pages with obsessively composed pictures. A teenager who believes she doesn't measure up could end up hurting herself—through anorexia, bulimia, cutting, or even suicide.

The rest of Proverbs 29:25 tells us that those who trust in the Lord are safe. There is safety in trusting the Lord with all things, including our physical appearance.

IDENTITY TRUTH

The lies we believe about beauty and outward appearance are often deeply imbedded in our minds and hearts. They can cause great damage if they are not challenged and corrected. And how can we do this? To correct and redirect our thinking about beauty, we must run to the place where God outlines our identity: his Word.

We can't tackle this subject without first defining what we mean by beauty or beautiful. Beauty by definition is "the quality or aggregate of qualities in a person or thing that gives pleasure to the senses or pleasurably exalts the mind or spirit."[3]

Have you ever seen something that takes your breath away, like the Swiss Alps or the clear blue sea? Or maybe it's a baby or a woman. Beauty—even physical human beauty—isn't sinful. It's God's idea in the first place—his gift to his beloved children. But in a world that has been turned upside down by sin, marred by the fall, our idea of beauty and our response to it so often becomes warped. To undo those distortions, we must rethink our idea of what is truly beautiful.

Beauty starts with God. God is the Creator of the universe, and he defines what is beautiful.

When we think about the beauty found in Scripture, we see outward beauty referenced. God created a breathtakingly beautiful world filled with externally beautiful people, and he does not shy away from drawing our attention to them (see Gen. 29:17, 1 Sam. 25:3, Song of Solomon, and so on).

However, the Bible makes it clear that outward beauty is not the essence of who God is or what he wants from his people. It's not his primary standard of beauty. The true beauty of God is his holiness, his righteousness, and his purity.

Pastor and author A.W. Tozer puts it this way:

Holy is the way God is. To be holy he does not conform to a standard. He is that standard. . . . Because he is

---

3   "Beauty," Merriam-Webster, accessed March 8, 2018,
     https://www.merriam-webster.com/dictionary/
     beauty?utm_campaign=sd&utm_medium=serp&utm_source=jsonld.

holy, his attributes are holy; that is, whatever we think of as belonging to God must be thought of as holy."[4]

What does that tell us about the standards of beauty to which God calls us? Peter, writing to Christians in the Roman provinces of Asia Minor, gave us a hint: "Do not let your adorning be external—the braiding of hair and the putting on of gold jewelry, or the clothing you wear—but let your adorning be the hidden person of the heart with the imperishable beauty of a gentle and quiet spirit, which in God's sight is very precious" (1 Pet. 3:3–4).

In the first century jewelry signified wealth. So Peter was simply saying: don't be a show-off. Don't put a lot of time of energy on your outward appearance. Instead, let your beauty routine focus on developing the kind of gentle and quiet spirit that comes from trusting and fearing the Lord.

When describing a woman who possessed such a spirit, Peter used the example of Sarah, who lived with quiet courage and "did not fear anything that was frightening" (3:6)—including, we can assume, whether other people thought she was outwardly beautiful. That's the courage that God wants us to live in, a courage that comes from deep trust and confidence in the One who made us.

Clearly, God is focused on transforming the inner person. He wants our hearts. He wants to give us new hearts and a new purpose (Ezek. 3:26–28). That transformation will make us truly beautiful.

So, if our beautification is not to be external, but that of a hidden spirit, then there's something far more beautiful

---

4   A. W. Tozer, *Knowledge of the Holy: Knowing God Through His Attributes* (1961; repr. North Fort Myers, FL: Faithful Life Publishers, 2017), chap. 21, Kindle.

than the outward. And if God calls us to be holy as he is holy, then God's holiness is beautiful. And we know that our righteousness comes only from the righteousness of Christ, which leads us to the source of our true beauty—Jesus.

We have at least one hint in Scripture that the human Jesus might not have been outwardly attractive. Isaiah described the coming Messiah as someone who has "no form or majesty that we should look at him, and no beauty that we should desire him" (Isa. 53:3).

And yet Jesus is the image of the invisible God, "the radiance of the glory of God and the exact imprint of his nature" (Col. 1:15; Heb.1:3). How can he help but be infinitely beautiful, as God is beautiful?

Jesus is glorious! He is righteous and pure, and that is what makes him oh so beautiful. We were made to be in awe of that beauty—in the words of the psalmist, to "gaze upon the beauty of the Lord" (Ps. 27:4). That take-your-breath-away response to beautiful things is what we experience when we're awakened to the beauty of Christ.

If we're called to be like Jesus, then we're called to be beautiful as he is beautiful—to grow into our beautiful identity as his transformed people.

IDENTITY TRANSFORMED

Although the fall didn't wipe away beauty, as with all things, it affected it. Therefore, as we look to correct our views of beauty, remember that our outward selves are wasting away. Setting our eyes on the eternal helps transform our focus for today.

The older I get, the more I experience the reality of living in a fallen body. I ache in ways I didn't before. I look in the mirror and see lines and bags. My health isn't as easy to maintain. My hips . . . well, we aren't even going to dis-

cuss those. If beauty as the world defines it is all that there
is to strive for, then we're all in for quite a disappointing
end of life.

We may try every experimental procedure and beauty
treatment to prolong or prevent the inevitable. Nothing will
work in the long run. Botox and plastic surgery and healthy
eating and a lifetime of marathons cannot prevent our
inevitable fate. Like Adam in the Bible, we are dust and will
return to dust (Gen. 3:19). Any outward beauty we're blessed
with or manage to achieve in our lifetime will eventually
degrade and disappear.

Thankfully, God hasn't left us to that depressing fate.
We know that in time he will make all things new and that
what was once rife with disease and pain will rise into glory
with Christ. Paul connected the fall and our resurrection for
us when he wrote, "For as in Adam all die, so also in Christ
shall all be made alive. But each in his own order: Christ the
firstfruits, then at his coming those who belong to Christ"
(1 Cor. 15:22–23).

As if that weren't good news enough, Paul explained
that not only will we be with Christ but we will be like him:
"Our citizenship is in heaven, and from it we await a Savior,
the Lord Jesus Christ, who will transform our lowly body to
be like his glorious body, by the power that enables him even
to subject all things to himself" (Phil. 3:20–21).

Yes, God will make everything new, including us. He
will transform our bodies, the ones we are pulling and tuck-
ing and starving in an effort to make them beautiful. They
will be beautiful, pure, and glorious when he returns—un-
imaginably beautiful. We will never die again. Our beauty
will never fade. Most importantly, we will be without sin.

Our fallen and imperfect bodies are yet another way we
can look to Christ. Each ache and pain and droopy muscle
is another reminder that we have a Savior who is perfect in

beauty, and he is coming to get us—to raise us to a condition more glorious than we can imagine. In the meantime, by his grace, we can take our eyes off ourselves and fix them squarely on Jesus.

If we know life is not about pursuing a cultural "ideal" that God didn't create us to maintain, we can refocus our gaze on Christ and pursue that which the Lord did create us for. God created us for worship—for himself. We see just a glimpse of this purpose in Psalm 100:3: "Know that the LORD, he is God! It is he who made us, and we are his; we are his people, and the sheep of his pasture."

We are his! We are God's creation (Eph. 2:10). Each intricately designed cell, every single strand of hair—everything—was designed by God (Matt. 10:30), made for his glory (Isa. 43:7), and therefore intrinsically beautiful. But far more beautiful in his sight is the person we are becoming as we pursue holiness and follow Jesus in this world.

That doesn't mean we have to ditch all of our beauty products or stop going to the gym! We simply (or not so simply!) need to train our hearts and minds to focus on what we will be focused on for all eternity. Soon we will no longer have to ask the Lord that we may gaze upon his beauty. Soon we will be with him gazing and in awe for eternity.

In the meantime, we can rest knowing that God will finish that work in us (Phil. 1:6). The lies that our culture instills in us about beauty and the lies we tell ourselves don't have to control us. With his help, we can live in the truth that a "beautiful" face or a "perfect body" will never bring us the love and acceptance and self-worth we hunger for.

The only beautiful thing that will ever truly satisfy isn't a "thing" at all. It's a person—Jesus.

VERSE TO MEMORIZE

Do not let your adorning be external—the braiding of hair and the putting on of gold jewelry, or the clothing you wear—but let your adorning be the hidden person of the heart with the imperishable beauty of a gentle and quiet spirit, which in God's sight is very precious.

1 Peter 3:3–4

QUESTIONS FOR GROUP DISCUSSION

OPENING QUESTION: In what ways do you see the pursuit of beauty in our culture today? How does it affect the way we use our time, money, and energy?

1.   Why is beauty a good thing? What is the difference between celebrating or enjoying beauty and idolizing beauty?

2.   When you think of God, do you describe him as beautiful? READ PSALM 27:4, PSALM 96:6, AND ISAIAH 28:5. How do these verses describe God, and how do they affect your understanding of beauty?

3.   How does our quest for beauty extend beyond just our physical appearance? How does it affect how we view other people and our possessions?

4.   READ 2 KINGS 17:14–18.

    a.   How did the Israelites fall into idolatry?

    b.   According to this passage how does unbelief lead to idolatry? How does it lead to sin?

    c.   What are the consequences of idolatry?

    d.   In what ways is it a struggle for us to believe God that inner beauty (holiness, righteousness, goodness) is more important than outer beauty?

e. How is our unbelief the root of our idolatry of
    beauty? How does it lead us away from the Lord
    and into disobedience and sin?

f. What consequences do you think result from a
    misplaced idolatry of beauty?

5. How does our comparison with others interfere with
    our relationships with them? Have you ever struggled
    with jealousy or envy toward someone because of her
    beauty? How did that struggle affect your relationship
    with them?

6. How does the truth of the gospel calm our fears of not
    being accepted by others because we don't measure up
    to their standard of beauty?

7. READ I PETER 3:3–6.

    a. What would it look like practically to pursue the
        imperishable beauty of a gentle and quiet spirit?
        How would that affect your use of time, energy,
        and money?

    b. Why is it tempting to place our hope and trust in
        our outward appearance rather than in God? Why
        will the pursuit of worldly beauty ultimately fail
        to satisfy?

8. READ PHILIPPIANS 3:20. How does this verse encour-
    age you today?

9. Think of someone who might not be described as
    beautiful by the world's standards, yet her life beauti-

fully reflects Jesus. What shines forth from her life that makes her attractive in a way that is deeper and richer than other forms of beauty?

10. As you think back over the chapter, what particular truth resonated with you? How will you live differently in light of that new understanding?

CHAPTER 8

SERVANT: REAPING A REWARD

BETSY CHILDS HOWARD

Man is born to be a servant and a servant he must
be. Who shall be his master? That is the question.[1]
—Charles Spurgeon

It's Wednesday night. I've cooked dinner for the Bible study we host each week in our apartment. The meal is ready on time. As members arrive from their jobs around the city, they exclaim how "amazing" dinner smells, and it turns out to be tasty. The men help themselves to seconds, and the wom-

---

1   Charles Spurgeon, "Our Change of Masters," Spurgeon Gems & Other Treasures of God's Truth, https://www.spurgeongems.org/vols25-27/chs1482.pdf.

en again announce that it was "amazing." I think silently, *I love to serve!*

It's Thursday night. I've cooked dinner for my husband and myself. I got a late start because I forgot to buy fresh garlic at the store and had to go back. I turn the oven up, hoping the meal will cook faster. The kitchen is hot and I'm a bit sweaty, but we sit down to eat not too many minutes after I had planned. As I cut into my chicken breast, I see the sickening pink of an uncooked middle. I look over at my husband who is silently cutting around the center of his chicken breast. I start a passionate internal monologue of self-defense: "He has no idea how much I do for us. He takes me for granted. Our oven is not reliable. I do too much for our church. The fact that our chicken is raw is not my fault!"

These two scenarios encapsulate my love/hate relationship with serving. When serving makes me look good, it's rewarding. When my service is deficient (e.g. raw chicken) I get angry and want to blame someone. When my service is overlooked, I feel resentful and unappreciated.

IDENTITY THEFT

Most of the Christians I know take for granted that serving others is a good thing. After all, Jesus said, "But whoever would be great among you must be your servant, and whoever would be first among you must be your slave, even as the Son of Man came not to be served but to serve, and to give his life as a ransom for many" (Matt. 20:26b–28). Moreover, in some relationships we have no choice but to serve others, as when caring for small children or aging parents. But it's difficult to move from knowing you *should* serve to joyfully serving those who take you for granted.

There's a scene in *Downton Abbey* where Lady Sybil, the youngest daughter of an earl, asks Mrs. Patmore, the family cook, to teach her to bake a cake. With much guidance and help, she succeeds. Her mother comes upon the scene just as the cake is taken out of the oven. As she watches, tears of joy and pride fill her eyes. Her daughter has baked a cake!

In a sense, this is the scene I'm hoping for every time I perform an act of service for someone else. I want them to be grateful and to think well of me. Sometimes this happens, but often my service is received more like one of Mrs. Patmore's cakes. She's the family cook, and she bakes cakes every day because it's her job. She's a servant.

While we may agree that Christians should be servant-hearted, no one wants to be treated like a servant. "I'm not their servant," we mutter under our breath when we feel taken for granted by our family, boss, or coworkers. And we're not.

Servants are employed by one master but serve many others who are not their masters. In a house like Downton Abbey, a footman waits on everyone at the table, but his only master is the lord of the house. The good servant lives to please his master and to serve those the master assigns to his care.

It helps me to remember that, in terms of spiritual service, my only master is God. He has given me neighbors to serve for his sake. Pleasing other people is a good thing, but when I serve for their approval rather than God's, I put them in the place of the Master and forget my true identity: a servant of God.

IDENTITY TRUTH

There's a reason why it's so much harder to serve when people overlook our service or don't appreciate it. God designed us to seek approval. He created us to desire a reward for all our hard work. When we try to psych ourselves up to live

sacrificially without any hope of recognition, we aren't thinking the way God thinks. The scriptural motive for service
is the hope of blessing (John 13:12–17). Our problem is not
that we seek reward, but that we expect it to come from the
wrong people.

One of the best articulations of the biblical motive for
serving others is addressed to actual servants in Paul's letter
to the Colossians:[2]

> Bondservants, obey in everything those who are your
> earthly masters, not by way of eye-service, as peo-
> ple-pleasers, but with sincerity of heart, fearing the
> Lord. Whatever you do, work heartily, as for the Lord
> and not for men, knowing that from the Lord you will
> receive the inheritance as your reward. You are serving
> the Lord Christ. (Col. 3:22–24)

Imagine you're a first-century indentured servant. Day after
day, you wash your mistress's clothes in the river. You dry
them in the sun to bleach the natural fibers. You hope she
will notice the care you take to please her, but she never no-
tices. In fact, she takes out her bad moods on you by mocking
you and speaking harshly.

In this situation, you're faced with a choice. You could
stop trying so hard since you're never going to be appreciated. Or you could choose to do your best because you know

---

2   The Greek word translated "bondservant" is *doulos*. This word can be
translated as "slave" or "servant." The translation committee of the
English Standard Version chose "bondservant" in this instance to
signify that a *doulos* in New Testament times was not owned (as were
American chattel slaves), but instead indentured for a period of time
or until a set amount of debt had been repaid.

the Lord of all the earth will see your efforts and be pleased by them. You may discover ways to serve and benefit your mistress that she will never know. If so, you can take secret joy in your unrewarded excellence because you know the Lord will repay you.

What sort of reward can we expect from our Master? We've already read in Colossians 3 that we will receive an inheritance. We will be God's heirs. Furthermore, Jesus promises that those who serve him will be with him and honored by his Father: "If anyone serves me, he must follow me; and where I am, there will my servant be also. If anyone serves me, the Father will honor him" (John 12:25–26). Isn't honor what we crave when we serve? That's how God designed us, but we look for that honor from people who can't satisfactorily give it.

Perhaps you're thinking, doesn't our salvation in Christ apart from works make us Christ's heirs? It's absolutely true that we can only be made right with God through the shed blood of Jesus. His righteousness, not ours, gives us access into his presence (for more on this, see chapter 4 of this book). Yet over and over in the Bible, we're told that our actions in this life have consequences in the next. For example, we can store up treasure in heaven by giving away what we have on earth (Matt. 6:20).

Jesus warned, "Beware of practicing your righteousness before other people in order to be seen by them, for then you will have no reward from your Father who is in heaven" (Matt. 6:1). Buried in this warning is the glorious news that in the life to come, our Father will celebrate good deeds that go unnoticed on earth. Looking forward to this promised reward helps us embrace our identity as servants—and heirs—of God.

IDENTITY TRANSFORMED

What might it look like to live out a transformed identity
as a servant of God? To serve in the hope of honoring God
rather than rising in the estimation of others?

It might look like washing the coffee pot at work, week
after week, even though your coworkers have never noticed
or wondered how it stays clean.

It might be cheerfully visiting a relative with Alzhei-
mer's even though she doesn't recognize you and bitterly
complains her family has forgotten her.

It might mean serving a store-bought dessert to dinner
guests, even though no one was ever impressed by the ability
to buy a dessert.

It might look like volunteering on the cleanup crew for
a fundraiser even though you know the decorating crew is
more fun and earns more recognition.

It might mean gladly agreeing to watch your neighbor's
child even though the last time you watched her, the child
came down with a stomach virus, and your neighbor didn't
think it was a big deal or even seem appreciative.

Once we know we're serving the Lord rather than men
and women, we can stop worrying about whether we are un-
der-appreciated. We can stop focusing on whether our efforts
enhance our image and start concentrating on how we can
best meet the needs of our neighbors.

When we serve for the Lord's reward rather than the
appreciation of men and women, we will still have service
"fails," but they needn't send us into defensiveness or shake
our identity. You may do your roommate's laundry as a favor
and accidentally turn a white shirt pink. Or maybe you baked
a loaf of bread for a new mom, forgetting that she once told
you she has a wheat allergy. Your act of service may end up
lowering you in the estimation of the one you tried to serve.

In such a case, after apologizing from the heart and making whatever restoration you can, you can rest in the fact that you are a beloved, treasured heir of God, even if you appear incompetent before men.

What of those times when our service is warmly appreciated by those we serve? When your child tells you you're the best mommy in the world, or your coworker sends an email of commendation to your supervisor after you've gone the extra mile on a project? We can't live for these moments of being seen and appreciated, and we can't count on them to fuel our service. But we can rejoice in the glimpse they offer of the joy God takes in our service.

Jesus gave up the glory of heaven to become the servant of men by saving us from our sins. He was despised and rejected by those he came to serve. Yet he loved us to the end, and he received his reward: "Therefore God has highly exalted him and bestowed on him the name that is above every name . . . " (Phil. 2:9). Whether we are applauded or despised by those around us, we too can serve for the joy of our Master and enter into his great reward.

VERSE TO MEMORIZE

Whatever you do, work heartily, as for the Lord and not for men, knowing that from the Lord you will receive the inheritance as your reward. You are serving the Lord Christ.

Colossians 3:23–24

QUESTIONS FOR GROUP DISCUSSION

OPENING QUESTION: If you could have a personal assistant or servant to help you with one area of your life, what area would you choose?

1. Is the thought of being a servant a positive or negative idea to you? How does it change your perception of yourself to identify as a servant?

2. CONSIDER JOSHUA 1:1, DANIEL 3:26, LUKE 1:38, PHILIPPIANS 1:1, JAMES 1:1, AND REVELATION 15:3. What do you notice about how these leaders are described? How does this affect your understanding of both leadership and servanthood?

3. How does the stature or importance of the person you are serving affect your willingness to serve or your attitude while serving?

4. What are areas in your life that you serve, but people rarely notice or appreciate your efforts? In what ways is that difficult?

5. READ JOHN 13:1–17.

    a. How did Jesus serve his disciples? Why do you think he served them in this way?

    b. What did he command them to do?

    c. Why is it significant that Jesus also washed the feet of Judas? What does his example teach you?

d.   Jesus tells his disciples they will be blessed if they serve others. How have you experienced blessings as you have served others?

6.   When serving others, do you ever grumble and complain? Or perhaps believe the work you are being asked to do is somehow "beneath" you? How does it change your perspective (and attitude) to believe that your daily acts of service are for the Lord?

7.   READ PHILIPPIANS 2:1–10.

a.   What are we commanded to do in this passage?

b.   In what ways is Christ an example of service for us? Why is his example of service so meaningful?

c.   According to verses 9–11, what was the result of Christ's humility?

d.   How can we take encouragement in Christ's exaltation?

8.   Whom do you know as an example of service with joy and humility? What can you learn from their example? Is there a way you can encourage them in their service this week?

9.   How does knowing that God sees your labors and rewards them encourage you in the mundane or hidden places you serve?

10. As you think back over the chapter, what particular truth resonated with you? How will you live differently in light of that new understanding?

CHAPTER 9

WORSHIPER: SHINING BRIGHTLY IN THE DARKNESS

LINDSEY CARLSON

*The question is not whether you will worship,
but rather what you will worship—your glorious Creator or something He created.[1]*
—Paul David Tripp

Nestled off Interstate 35 on a stretch of Texas highway
between Austin and San Antonio, a large illuminated billboard with a red and yellow cartoon beaver named "Buc-ee"

---

[1]   Paul David Tripp, *New Morning Mercies: A Daily Gospel Devotional*
(Wheaton, IL: Crossway, 2014), November 25.

beckons road weary travelers to come and behold the world's largest convenience store. Like moths to a flame, tourists are drawn to come, see, and marvel at the 67,000-square-foot gas station. Past its 60 gas pumps and inside its welcoming storefront, customers can buy plates of Texas BBQ or fresh beef jerky, choose from 23 kinds of homemade fudge, peruse the aisles of custom "Buc-ee's" goodies like caramel-coated corn puff "Beaver Nuggets," and shop endless offerings of home decor and enough beaver emblazoned t-shirts, key-chains, koozies, and coolers to blow your mind. While the sheer size and the beaver gimmicks are certainly part of the draw, they're only part of what's built the loyal customer base and kept Buc-ee's thriving in 32 locations across Texas.

During an interview with *Forbes*, Buc-ee's founder Beaver Aplin poses proudly for a picture before the company's *real* main attraction—their toilets. Forbes author Peter Carbonara writes, "The insight that runs beneath the rise of Buc-ee's convenience stores is this: You can get a lot of people to pull off the highway and spend money if you guarantee them an immaculate place in which to heed the call of nature. As one Buc-ee's billboard proclaims, "Your Throne Awaits. Fabulous Restrooms—32 miles."[2] Aplin reports his company's $275 million in revenue last year rides on the cleanliness of those toilets and the name he's built on their porcelain.

Pause for a moment and reflect on this strange fame. We're talking about a multi-million-dollar business model built around *toilets*. We are a people who've grown accus-

---

2   Peter Carbonara, "Buc-ees Game of Porcelain Thrones," *Forbes Magazine*, September 5, 2017, https://www.forbes.com/sites/petercarbonara/2017/08/22/buc-ees-game-of-porcelain-thrones/#2ea3ae2b7626.

tomed to the advertisement of the average and the overblowing of the ordinary.

It should come as no surprise that we've learned to build a name for ourselves too. We are bombarded with western culture's admonishment to garnish attention for ourselves. "If in order to be loved you must be known," it says, "then you must work harder to be seen." In a world of roughly 7 billion people, we've noticed it's the mesmerizing, not the mediocre who stand out. But if we leave our life's ad campaign in the hands of culture and our natural instincts, our billboard will play out like a message straight from 2 Timothy 3:2—revealing we are lovers of self, lovers of money, proud, and arrogant. We are inclined to seek our own interests, not those of Jesus Christ (Phil. 2:21). In order to let our light shine before men (Matt. 5:16) in the way Christ intended, we will need to evaluate who or what it is that we're calling attention to.

IDENTITY THEFT

God will not give his glory to another (Is. 48:11), writes the prophet Isaiah. Yet we are a people who delight in our own glory. It's not only for the name of Christ that we want to *be* excellent wives, doting moms (but not too doting), successful career women, loyal friends, fashionable decorators, beautiful and fit stewards of our bodies, and compassionate social-justice advocates. We also want to be *recognized* for these accomplishments *for our own sake*. We want to be *praised* for our unique insight, brilliant creativity, selfless sacrifice, and dogged persistence. *Sought out* for our excellence or expertise. We may not want to admit it, but we want to be *worshiped*. To that end, we've become public-relations managers tirelessly crafting our own lives into personal ad-campaigns to sell the product of ourselves.

Marriage, parenting, careers, hobbies, spiritual gifts—
we're tempted to use them all for our own good and gain.
"Make much of me!" is the battle cry of our flesh. The sin
nature seductively sways us to build a name for *ourselves.* And
if we're not careful, we'll go about cultivating any fragment
of truth into an opportunity for selfish gain. We become bill-
boards of self and invite others to come, see, and marvel. Like
the Romans, we exchange the glory of the immortal God for
images resembling mortal man (Rom. 1:23).

We are, by nature, worshipers. Instead of worshiping
the Creator, we choose to worship self. D.A. Carson writes,
"At the heart of the Fall is the self-love that destroys our
God-centeredness. Implicitly, of course, all failure to worship
God is neither more nor less idolatry. Because we are finite,
we will inevitably worship something or someone."[3]

Our failure to worship God, and instead worship
ourselves, is an attempt to eclipse the glory of God and steal
praise only ever intended for him. When we do so, we take
our place alongside the rebellious Israelites who worshiped a
metal image, exchanged the glory of God for the image of an
ox, and forgot their Savior (Psa. 106:20–21). This is *not* who
we were created to be. "Self-worshiper" is not our true self.
Elevating ourselves and our God-given gifts and abilities for
selfish gain is not only sinful idolatry, it's false advertisement
to a watching world. *You* are not the glorious One worthy of
all praise and honor.

---

3   D.A. Carson, "Worship Under the Word," in *Worship by the Book*, ed.
    D. A. Carson (Grand Rapids: Zondervan, 2002), 34.

IDENTITY TRUTH

While our worship is often misplaced, our desire to worship is wonderful. We were created to be people of praise. However, we often set our sights too low for *what* we worship. We take to social media to praise our children's crayon scribbling, the shiplap wall our husband installed in the laundry room, and the tasty food from the new local restaurant we found on our date night. We attend concerts where we unashamedly whistle, clap, and scream as our favorite singer belts out the lyrics of our favorite song. We give our attention and loyalty to football teams by handing over our time and money. We are a people purposed for praise, but we often misdirect our efforts.

The writer of 1 Chronicles clues us into the object of all good and right worship: "Ascribe to the LORD the glory due his name; bring an offering and come before *him*! Worship the LORD in the splendor of holiness; tremble before *him*, all the earth; yes, the world is established; it shall never be moved" (1 Chron. 16:29–30, italics added). Even "the heavens declare the glory of God, and the sky above proclaims his handiwork" (Ps. 19:1). What does your life proclaim?

Each morning is an opportunity to praise God as the giver of life. Does your life shout "God is my creator! I am the clay, the work of his hand!" (Isa. 64:8)? Are you overwhelmed by the gift of your beating heart, the breath in your lungs, the blood pumping through your veins, and your intricate immune system? They are all part of his glorious design. Isn't life itself, an invitation to worship him for how wonderfully he made you?

Not only did God create us, in Christ, he's redeemed us. Through his Word, his Son, and his Spirit, we've been afforded a front row seat to view endless examples of his kindness and mercy, so that in response, we might praise *him*.

Beholding his glory we proclaim, "There is none holy like the Lord: for there is none besides [him]; there is no rock like our God" (1 Sam. 2:2). He is redeemer, savior, and friend. It would be the understatement of eternity to say he is matchless. God is bigger, better, and far more worthy of our worship than the hair products, blenders, podcast personalities, and lesser trinkets we sometimes lavish our love upon.

God is not only worthy of our worship, he commands it. The first two commandments offer guardrails that guide the object of our affections: worship God alone and do not worship idols. He is by self-admission *a jealous God* (Ex. 20:2–5), not satisfied to sit in the back seat of our lives. Worship is much more than an hour on a Sunday morning, the two-minute prayer whispered over meals, or time spent listening to a Christian radio station on the way to work. Worship is more than the songs we sing, or the services we attend. It isn't constrained to closed eyes and hands in the air. Worship isn't something we occasionally *do*. Worship is a posture of life—an overflow of a heart filled with gratitude and praise for the King who sits on the throne, the only One worthy of all the praise we can bring.

This posture of awe, reverence, and humble submission can happen anywhere: in your home, in your car, at work, in the line at the grocery store, or on the treadmill. Worship is simply saying, "Because you are worthy and because I love you, I will respond with my life."

You can worship God by rising early to meet with him in his Word, by speaking kindly to your children, by encouraging an anxious friend, forgiving a co-worker, or sharing a meal with the rough-around-the-edges woman you'd rather avoid. Sometimes worship will be through words prayed: "thank you," "help," or "forgive me." Sometimes worship will be silent: quietly observing God's beauty in nature, noting his strength in your weakness, or his mercy on display in your relationships. By directing your praise to God, you'll experience your true identity as a worshiper, a joyful privilege and delight.

IDENTITY TRANSFORMED

We're called to play a role in declaring God's "glory among the nations, his marvelous works among all the peoples" (Ps. 96:3), by "proclaim[ing] the excellencies of him who called [us] out of darkness into his marvelous light" (1 Pet. 2:9). Declaring ourselves worthy of praise and adoration makes us false advertisers, selling a counterfeit good that leads others further into darkness and away from the cross of Christ.

Rather than worshipers of self, we're created to be proclamation people. We have enormous potential to reflect the glory of God when we're living in tune with what's ultimately true and beautiful. We're made in the image of God, uniquely positioned to demonstrate his attributes to a watching world. As followers of Christ our lives are intended to advertise the awesome and overwhelmingly extraordinary grace of God. Upon salvation, the sinner—pardoned by God, redeemed by Christ, and led by the Spirit of God himself—becomes a living, breathing announcement of the glorious splendors of the triune God.

We who have received salvation know something exceptional and infinitely worthy of proclamation:

> For what we proclaim is not ourselves, but Jesus Christ as Lord, with ourselves as your servants for Jesus' sake. For God, who said 'Let light shine out of darkness,' has shone in our hearts to give the light of the knowledge of the glory of God in the face of Jesus Christ. (2 Cor. 4:5–6)

Instead of false advertisers proclaiming the glories of ourselves, let us embrace our identity as people of proclamation who live and breathe to exalt Jesus.

We're called to carry the light of Jesus into the dark and needy world. Jesus's command to go into all the world and "make disciples of all nations" (Matt. 28:19) was intended to be fulfilled by word-of-mouth witnesses whose hearts have been transformed by the power of the gospel. We who once "walked in darkness have seen a great light" (Isa. 9:2), and as citizens of the coming kingdom of heaven we share this light with others.

Our desire to steal God's glory lurks constantly in the background. Paul asks the Corinthian church in 2 Corinthians 3:1, "Are we beginning to commend ourselves again?" The tendency toward self-accolade is dangerous because it threatens the testimony of believers: "You yourselves are our letter of recommendation, written on our hearts, to be known and read by all. And you show that you are a letter from Christ delivered by us, written not with ink but with the Spirit of the living God, not on tablets of stone but on tablets of human hearts" (2 Cor. 3:2–3).

Christ's work in our lives becomes a living, breathing testament to the Spirit's work. Consumed with self-glory, we will not focus on our evangelistic mission, because we cannot simultaneously worship both God and self. If we hope to rightly worship God, we lay down our own glory in favor of his.

As people come and go throughout your life, what light attracts them? What are you showcasing? Are people compelled to come, to see, and to marvel at *you*, or at *Christ in you*? In this dark world, don't be just another pit stop exalting something as ordinary as a bathroom and selling t-shirts and koozies with pictures of your own smiling face. Leave that to Buc-ee's. Instead, use your life to shine as a light in the world, "holding fast to the word of life" (Phil. 2:15–16).

Christ is spectacular. He is *actually* due all praise and honor. Proclaim his name. Point others to him. Settle for nothing less than the worship of the One who's truly worthy of affection and awe. Use everything at your disposal to be a gigantic, illuminated billboard of God's glory and the mercy of Christ. In the process you'll draw road-weary life travelers to the only source of wonder and point them to the only One worthy of our worship.

VERSE TO MEMORIZE

*And Jesus answered him, "It is written, 'You shall wor-
ship the Lord your God, and him only shall you serve.'"*

Luke 4:8

QUESTIONS FOR GROUP DISCUSSION

OPENING QUESTION: How do you see worship in our culture when you consider the way we celebrate sports, entertainment, and famous people?

1.   In what ways does our culture present more opportunities than ever to engage in self-worship or self-promotion?

2.   How does our desire to be noticed and appreciated often lead us to exhaustion and weariness?

3.   READ ROMANS 1: 16–23 AND PSALM 19: 1–3.

   a.   Why should all people worship God?

   b.   What happens when people worship created things rather than their Creator?

   c.   How does our understanding of the gospel encourage our worship?

4.   When you hear the word "worship" what images usually come to mind? Compare your answer with Romans 12:1–2. How does this passage expand your understanding of worship?

5.   What in your life are you tempted to worship in place of God? Think of the places or people you hope, trust, and delight in—what captures your affections more than God does?

6. How does what we worship affect: What we talk about? What we spend our time doing? What we spend our money on?

7. READ JOHN 4:21–26. What does it mean to worship God in spirit and in truth?

8. How does worship lead us to be proclamation people who faithfully obey Jesus's command in Matthew 28:19–20: "Go therefore and make disciples of all nations, baptizing them in the name of the Father and of the Son and of the Holy Spirit, teaching them to observe all that I have commanded you"?

9. As you think back over the chapter, what particular truth resonated with you? How will you live differently in light of that new understanding?

CHAPTER 10

CITIZEN: LONGING FOR HOME

JEN POLLOCK MICHEL

Most people, if they had really learned to look into their own hearts, would know that they do want, and want acutely, something that cannot be had in this world.[1]
—C. S. Lewis

We drove the nine hours to Toronto from Chicago in dreary mid-winter. Because my husband had been offered a short-term position in the city, our family was temporarily moving. We needed to rent a house and find a school for our kids before that relocation, so our family was visiting for a long weekend. One morning, after touring the elementary school

---

1   C. S. Lewis, *Mere Christianity*, in *The Complete C.S. Lewis Signature Classics* (New York: HarperCollins, 2002), 113.

and meeting with administrators, we took the subway down-town; our children emerged from Union Station wide-eyed into the bustle of Canada's largest city. Across the street, a cavalcade of dark SUVS idled in front of Toronto's Fairmont Royal York Hotel. Black-suited security personnel stood at attention. A crowd gathered outside the revolving doors of the hotel, and with them, we fell into the hushed expectancy of seeing someone famous.

Then my son began to whine inopportunely: "I have to go to the bathroom."

"Just a few more minutes," I reassured. But my dancing little boy was not to be put off. We dodged into a local restaurant. By the time we'd returned, the Very Important Person had driven away. Among the smattering of people who remained hunched over their phones, I approached one woman to ask, "Who just came out of the hotel?"

"Stephen Harper," she said, then returned to her phone. The kids tugged anxiously at my legs. "Who's Steven Harper, Mom?"

I backed away, then bent to whisper, "Let me google it." Stephen Harper, as the kids and I would learn, was the prime minister of Canada.

That was 2011; we're on our second prime minister now. The two or three years we had planned on living in Canada have quickly become seven—enough time to verse us more adequately in Canadian politics. But as each year has obliged to ask and answer the question if we planned to stay, "home" has become a slippery kind of word. On the other side of this international border, I've wondered: Is home the place of departure? Is home what you leave behind, the place you plan to return to when adventure's been spent? Or is home the place of arrival, even if it's a borrowed city and you're the tenant with an absentee landlord?

In 2016, Ikea surveyed 12,000 people in 12 global cities, asking respondents to answer this question: "What makes a home a home?" Their answers, despite dramatic demographic differences, were strikingly similar.[2]

Comfort.

Safety.

Belonging.

Love.

Home is the nagging ache of the human existence. We want to be settled somewhere safe; we want to be sheltered from impermanence. All of us are driven to find the place that knows us by name and receives us unconditionally. As Dorothy tried finding her way back to Kansas, she said it best: "There's no place like home."

How does the gospel make sense of this longing for home?

IDENTITY THEFT

Naomi and her husband, Elimelech, were expatriates in a season of famine (Ruth 1:1). With their two sons, Mahlon and Chilion, they left Bethlehem because the city of bread had left them starving. I imagine that they, like my own family, planned for temporary stay in Moab—a "sojourn," as the biblical writer calls it. But as we know, clouds of misfortune darkened and descended. Elimelech died; years later, after their marriages to Moabite women, Mahlon and Chilion died, too. Home, in Naomi's story, turned out to be as fragile as a robin's egg.

---

2   "Life at Home Report," Ikea, accessed December, 2016, http://lifeathome.ikea.com/explore/.

It's ironic then to hear Naomi's rebuke to her daugh-
ters-in-law, Ruth and Orpah, who insisted on following
her back to Bethlehem when she heard the news that God
was feeding his people again. Don't return with me, she told
them. I have no husband, no sons. Even if I were to have a
husband this very night and conceive a son, you'd surely not
wait till they were of age to marry them! "Go, return each
of you to her mother's house . . . The LORD grant that you
may find rest, each of you in the house of her husband!"
(Ruth 1:8–9).

I can't help but find it surprising that though Naomi's
story of marriage and motherhood hadn't been a fairy tale of
happily-ever-rest, she wished the illusion on her daughters-
in-law. She told them to find a home in the arms of new
husbands—as if marriage and a minivan could ever console
our deepest longings for home.

We're fools to put our ultimate hopes in things that
don't last.

The longing for home is a human longing. What's also
invariably human are the ways we look to satisfy our longings
apart from Christ. The heart, John Calvin wrote, is an idol
factory, and it's producing widgets around the clock. We feel
the longing for home, but rather than understanding God as
its true source, we translate home exclusively as a narrative of
marriage or motherhood. *Rest in the arms of a husband!* Or, we
feel the longing for home and try making good on its promises with roaring fires, rustic paneled bedrooms, and elegant
tables, adorned with a single orchid. *Rest in a glossy picture
on Pinterest!* To be sure, marriage and motherhood, even a
well-appointed kitchen, are good gifts, but they are not the
truest, most lasting reality of home as we know it through
the gospel. These are gifts with expiration dates, and they will
inevitably leave us restless for a home that will not suffer loss.

Our desires for home are real. The misfortune is that we try temporarily soothing them. "Probably earthly pleasures were never meant to satisfy [my desire], but only to arouse it, to suggest the real thing," C. S. Lewis wrote. "If that is so, I must take care, on the one hand, never to despise, or be unthankful for, those earthly blessings, and on the other, never to mistake them for the something else of which they are only a kind of copy or echo or mirage. I must keep alive in myself the desire for my true country . . . I must make it the main object of life to press on to the other country and to help others do the same."[3] Home can be enjoyed in this life—but only as appetizer of the coming feast.

As we follow the yellow brick road of Scripture, we find our way to God's permanent promise of home.

IDENTITY TRUTH

According to Scripture, *rest* is, in one sense, biblical short-hand for *home*. In the Genesis 1 account of creation, God finished his six days of work and rested on the seventh day. It's not simply that God was catching his breath from a long week of work. God's rest was an act of enthronement. In ancient literature, it was understood that "deity rests in a temple, and only in a temple."[4] To read the story of creation in this way tells us that the earth wasn't simply a home for humanity; it was also home for God. When God made the world, he never intended to stand at a distance, a spectator to the domestic action. Rather, he was intent on opening the circle of his own self-giving love to his children. He was the

---

3   Lewis, *Mere Christianity*, 114.
4   John Walton, *The Lost World of Genesis One* (Downers Grove, IL: IVP Academic, 2009), 71.

first homemaker, and he had generously brought humanity to his table. The great tragedy, of course, is that those first children (and all who've come after them) have been greedy for someone else's food. Because of sin, we've lost home. We've been looking for it ever since.

But the gospel is the good news that God did not leave his people to exile. We see this good news played out in the drama of Israel's story. Making good on his promises of home to Abraham, God delivered his people from slavery in Egypt to a land flowing with milk and honey. It was to be a land of rest: rest from their wandering and rest from their enemies. He would settle them in their new home by an act of sheer grace, just as he had done in the garden. Don't forget my goodness, he said, when I give you "great and good cities that you did not build, and houses full of all good things that you did not fill and cisterns that you did not dig, and vineyards and olive trees that you did not plant" (Deut. 6:10–11). Theirs was a home-sweet-home, given by grace. But tragically, like the garden, it, too, was eventually forfeited by sin, and God's people were set to wandering again.

Into the despair of homesickness the prophets spoke: God's scattered people would be gathered. God would bring his children home.

After four centuries of what seemed to be silence from God, a new light dawned in Israel's story. The God who longed to share a home with his people put on flesh and "tabernacled" among his people (John 1:14). If creation had been the first temple God built for himself, Jesus's body was the final temple: destroyed and raised up in three days (John 2:19). And if creation had been the first home God built for humanity, Jesus's body was a promise for all the prodigals: that though we have all traveled to a distant country, spending our money to feast at someone else's table, we have a patient father watching the road. He hasn't given up on his desire to extend welcome.

This is the good news of the gospel: the sin that estranges us from our home in God is defeated. Salvation cannot be likened to an impersonal bank transaction, as if the only matter of consequence is that our ledger of guilt has been wiped clean. We're reconciled to the Father and set down as guest of honor at his feast! The very good home that we left behind in Genesis 3—that home we can't help but missing—is restored to us because of the person and work of Jesus. Through Christ, we have unobstructed access to the Father today and bright hope for a better world tomorrow. Every promise of home finds its yes in Christ (2 Cor. 1:20).

"Father of all, we give you thanks and praise, that when we were still far off you met us in your Son and brought us home."[5]

IDENTITY TRANSFORMED

How then shall we live? This is always the practical question on the other side of every theological truth. If the gospel is promising me a home with Christ, what does that mean in my everyday reality?

I used to think that embracing the truest reality of *home*—both as a present reality and also a future inheritance—meant detachment from the world. But I find the words of Paul in 1 Timothy to helpfully correct that assumption. Addressing the wealthy women and men in Ephesus, Paul tells them (strangely, in my opinion) that God "richly

5   Leland Rykand, Jim Wilhoit, Tremper Longman, Colin Duriez, Douglas Penney, and Daniel G. Reid, *Dictionary of Biblical Imagery* (Downers Grove, Ill: InterVarsity Press, 1998), 393.

provides us with everything to enjoy" (1 Tim. 6:17). In other words, not every pleasure in this life must be a guilty one. We can receive everything as if straight from the pockets of God—even a family and an earthly home.

But Paul didn't end his instruction there, and we're not so easily off the hook. After he commended the Ephesians' holy enjoyment, generosity, and contentment, he reminded them that their orientation to this world must involve a hardy dose of realism. They needed to know the difference between the temporary and the permanent, the earthly and the eternal. Whatever you do, he wrote, "take hold of that which is truly life" (1 Tim. 6:19). These words Paul wrote to Timothy echo those of Jesus, who in the Sermon on the Mount, cautioned against greed. "Do not lay up for yourselves treasures on earth, where moth and rust destroy and where thieves break in and steal, but lay up for yourselves treasures in heaven, where neither moth nor rust destroys and where thieves do not break in and steal" (Matt. 6:19–20). There is only one way to take hold of the life to come: it's by investing our treasure in the unseen reality of eternity. In no uncertain terms, our money (and our calendars) tell us what home story we're living.

In the book of Hebrews, we have examples of suffering saints who were sustained by the promise of God's eternal home. And they weren't simply grinning-and-bearing it until death swept them into glory; they had even "joyfully accepted the plundering of [their] property since [they] knew that [they themselves] had a better possession and an abiding one" (Heb. 10:34). Persecuted because of Christ, they had thrown open their doors to the people who would strip them of their material belongings. They held home in this life loosely. There was nothing in this life they couldn't lose. Home, as the gospel promises it, is rest from the chronic anxiety that this life must be good to us.

These saints suffered well because they knew the true story of home, and it helped them orient their desires rightly. This world, disappointing at best, cruel at worst, wasn't ever meant to satisfy their deepest longings. They were expatriates in a foreign country, and they lived with the inevitable sense of dislocation. They acknowledged "they were strangers and exiles on the earth. For people who speak thus make it clear that they are seeking a homeland . . . They desire a better country, that is, a heavenly one. Therefore God is not ashamed to be called their God, for he has prepared for them a city" (Heb. 11:13–14, 16). Faith is the way that we, along with them, practice waiting on a better world—the Sabbath rest of God (Heb. 4:9).

As it turns out, in God's story, home is, in one sense, a borrowed city. We're all tenants in this life, and there's a great freedom in the way we can live a joyful open-handedness in the here-and-now. None of us knows how long we're staying. And in another sense, with both the garden and the new Jerusalem in view, home is also the place we leave and the place to which we return. It's nostalgia and memory; it's anticipation, too. Home is the two magnetic poles of the human story—and the open invitation of God.

There's always enough room at God's table. Christ says, *Welcome home.*

VERSE TO MEMORIZE

But as it is, they desire a better country, a heavenly one. Therefore God is not ashamed to be called their God, for he has prepared for them a city.

Hebrews 11:16

QUESTIONS FOR GROUP DISCUSSION

OPENING QUESTION: How do you see a longing for home in books, movies, and magazines? Is this an American experience, or do you see it across cultures?

1. In what ways do we attempt to create perfect homes, both physically and relationally? How can this pursuit grow idolatrous at times?

2. What words would you use to describe your own desires for home? How would you describe the home you are trying to create?

3. In what ways do we conflate our identity with our home? How do we allow our physical homes to define or represent us? How do we allow our marital or motherhood status to do the same? What problems arise when we place our identity in our earthly homes?

4. READ PHILIPPIANS 3:17–21.

    a. Paul contrasts those who are citizens of heaven with those who walk as enemies of Christ. What are the characteristics of each?

    b. How would we live differently if our identity were firmly rooted in our heavenly home? What would it look like to spend our time and efforts for that kingdom?

5. C. S. Lewis writes, "I must keep alive in myself the desire for my true country . . . I must make it the main object of life to press on to the other country and to

help others do the same." How can we encourage a desire for our true home in both ourselves and also in others?

6.   READ EPHESIANS 2:19–21 AND I PETER 2:9–12.

    a.   What encouraging truths do you learn about your identity from these two passages?

    b.   In what ways are we "no longer strangers and aliens" and at the same time "sojourners and exiles"? What does it look like to live as both?

    c.   Read Hebrews 11:13–16. What can we learn from saints before us about how to live as "strangers and exiles"?

7.   Consider this quote from Marshall Segal: "God not only knit you together in your mother's womb; he also sovereignly orchestrated all the places you would call home—the periods and boundaries of your 'dwelling place.' You do not have a home by accident. Your home is an invitation from God to seek God, and a commission from God to help others seek God."[6] How does this quote encourage you to use your home, even when "home" may not be in a city you prefer, or may not be full of the family you envisioned?

---

6   Marshall Segal, "God Chose This Home for You," Desiring God, December 13, 2017, https://www.desiringgod.org/articles/god-chose-this-home-for-you.

8.   READ 2 CORINTHIANS 5:1–9.

    a.   How does this passage illuminate the temporary nature of our earthly dwellings?

    b.   How does knowing that something better is coming allow us to be of good courage and live hopeful lives in the midst of our groaning and longing?

9.   As you think back over the chapter, what particular truth resonated with you? How will you live differently in light of that new understanding?

TGC

THE GOSPEL COALITION

The Gospel Coalition is a fellowship of evangelical churches deeply committed to renewing our faith in the gospel of Christ and to reforming our ministry practices to conform fully to the Scriptures. We have committed ourselves to invigorating churches with new hope and compelling joy based on the promises received by grace alone through faith alone in Christ alone.

We desire to champion the gospel with clarity, compassion, courage, and joy—gladly linking hearts with fellow believers across denominational, ethnic, and class lines. We yearn to work with all who, in addition to embracing our confession and theological vision for ministry, seek the lordship of Christ over the whole of life with unabashed hope in the power of the Holy Spirit to transform individuals, communities, and cultures.

Join the cause and visit *TGC.org* for fresh resources that will equip you to love God with all your heart, soul, mind, and strength, and to love your neighbor as yourself.

Also Available from
The Gospel Coalition

Made in the USA
Monee, IL
07 June 2021